CARDCRAFT

Adrienne and Bert Holtje

CARDCRAFT

*Twenty-two techniques
for making your own
greeting cards and notepaper*

CHILTON BOOK COMPANY Radnor, Pennsylvania

Copyright © 1978 by Adrienne Holtje and Bert Holtje
All Rights Reserved
Published in Radnor, Pennsylvania, by Chilton Book Company
and simultaneously in Don Mills, Ontario, Canada
by Thomas Nelson & Sons, Ltd.
Manufactured in the United States of America

Library of Congress Cataloging in Publication Data
    Holtje, Adrienne.
      Cardcraft.

      (Chilton's creative crafts series)
      1. Greeting cards.   2. Stationery.   I. Holtje,
Herbert, joint author.   II. Title.   III. Title:
Notepaper.
TT872.H64   1978   745.59′4   78-17266
ISBN 0-8019-6655-8
ISBN 0-8019-6656-6 pbk.

1 2 3 4 5 6 7 8 9 0   7 6 5 4 3 2 1 0 9 8

Contents

CARDCRAFT

Introduction

When the U. S. Postal Service created a stamp in honor of Louis Prang in 1975, they were really saying thanks to the one person who has done more for the sale of stamps than any other American. Louis Prang is considered the father of the American Christmas card!

When Prang first started to print his cards in 1874 in Roxbury, Massachusetts, they were elaborate lithographs. Some of his designs often required as many as twenty different colors. However, the idea for the mass-produced greeting card didn't originate with Prang. Fifteenth-century wood engravers were producing inscribed prints, and the chances are that the idea existed even before this.

But to think of greeting cards only in terms of the mass mailings people make at special holidays is to miss the point. The history of the greeting card is really told in the cards made by individuals for special occasions. The handmade Valentines our children make in school today are inspired by the same feeling that motivated the children in the time of Queen Anne to hand-letter cards to their parents. Each English child tried to show with succeeding cards how his or her handwriting had improved from the previous year. Think of the parents of today who collect and enjoy each holiday card made by their children.

This book was written for everybody—

> —the artist who can create designs, but would like to know more about the reproduction techniques
> —the person with limited artistic ability who would like to be able to make one or a hundred cards
> —the teacher who would like to help students make special cards
> —and all individuals who feel that just once it might be nice to make a card that says just what they feel.

Making greeting cards is an art and a craft at the same time. Each chapter in this book describes an entirely different technique, and each is illustrated with step-by-step instructions. If you like, you not only can use the methods we describe for making cards and adapt them to your own design, but you can also copy the specific designs and illustrations we have created. We have included a collection of additional shapes, patterns, and illustrations in chapter 25, but you'll have more fun if you try to develop your own ideas.

Whether you plan to make one special card or many for a holiday greeting, you will find the artistic inspiration as well as the craft skills described in this book. We hope that you will enjoy making your own cards and discover the pleasure you can give and get when you use your hands and heart to do something special for someone.

Tools and Materials 1

How to select and use them,
plus how to make a French fold
and other useful information

When you decide to make your own greeting cards, you have something to say to someone. Whether it's "Happy Birthday" to one person, or "Merry Christmas" to many, the motivation is the same. You can make one card with something as simple as a felt marking pen, or you can make many cards with silk screen.

Whatever your intent, your ambition should be in keeping with your abilities. A person with some art training might elect to create a watercolor card, but one with little more than the desire to send a cheery greeting can do very well with scissors and a few scraps of paper. In other words, work with a medium and technique that you can handle to produce the kind of personal greeting you will be proud of.

Everyone, regardless of training or talent, will be able to make some very presentable cards from the instructions in the chapters that follow. Every technique has been thoroughly researched and tested. Those of you who have some artistic skills can adapt and modify the techniques to suit your needs and abilities.

But everyone will need to know a little about the tools and materials that are used to make greeting cards. Each tool and material we use in this book was chosen because we felt it was best for the specific project. The tools and materials called for are all readily available at office and art supply stores, variety stores, or other common retail stores. Some materials may seem odd, such as the meat package Styrofoam used for block printing, but all are readily accessible and are best-suited to the technique involved.

Here are the materials we have used throughout the book. But, remember, you do not need everything for every project. Each chapter has a list of the specific materials to be used in that project. In one chapter, the list is as short as some colored tissue paper, glue, and a pair of scissors.

3

Tools

Pencils. Use a soft pencil, 2B to 4B, for sketching, and a hard one for transferring a design with carbon or transfer paper. 4H and 6H are hard pencils that should be part of the cardmaker's kit.

Erasers. A kneaded eraser can be scrunched into any shape you want; it's ideal for getting into tight spots. A block of art gum is great for general cleaning of pencil marks and finger prints, and it can be used on fabric as well as on paper.

Pens. A crow quill pen can be very useful for fine line ink drawing. The nib has a flexible point with a tubular shaft that fits in a special holder. Perhaps the most adaptable lettering instrument is the Speed Ball pen. There are many point styles available, and it is handy for drawing as well as lettering. Both pens are usually sold in art supply stores.

Pen markers. Marking pens are some of the handiest tools you can have. Get a black one with a fine point for outlining, and others in the colors you plan to use on your cards. These pens are available in a range of tip sizes. If you have large areas to cover, get a marker with a wide tip. Some of the inks are water soluble, and others are permanent. Where you may be using other materials with the pen marker, it pays to make a compatability test. For example, if you plan to use a pen with water-based ink to embellish a card to be decorated with the water and oil technique (chapter 8), draw on the paper with the pen and test it in the water before making the card. If the water dissolves the marking, you will have to do the pen marking after the oil and water part of the card has been completed. And, if you plan to spray a card with a finish such as varnish or Krylon, test the colors with the finish first.

Cutting tools. Perhaps the best way to cut paper is with an X-acto knife. This tool is adaptable and you can switch to a number of different style blades. However, the best general blade for the cardmaker is a no. 11. The X-acto is the perfect knife to use for cutting stencils. Ordinary paper scissors will be needed in most of the projects, and you will find it helpful to have a pair of manicure scissors for intricate cutting. Not absolutely necessary, but helpful, will be a pair of dressmaker's pinking shears. These scissors leave a sawtooth edge when they cut. A paper cutter is also helpful, but not absolutely essential.

If you are going to make any block prints, you will need a set of linoleum cutting tools. These are small chisels with blades made in a variety of shapes. Get a set with a selection of blades ranging from narrow to wide.

Drawing and cutting aids. A steel straight edge is better than a conventional ruler. With the steel edge, you will be able to cut a neater line and there is no chance of knicking the edge if you slip. A steel straight edge is also easier to use when inking a line. A triangle is also very helpful. Whether it is a 30° - 60° or a 45° angle is of little importance. The right-angle portion is most often used. You might consider getting a template for drawing circles. This eliminates the need for a compass, but it does limit you to the size circles on the form.

Brushes. A good watercolor brush is important, so buy the best you can get. Using a child's paint brush or an inexpensive one will be more trouble than it's worth. An inexpensive brush is fine for use with shellac, acrylic medium, or wax, though. A stencil brush is handy to have, too. This brush is cut flat on the end and has stiff bristles. Apart from its main use with stencils, it can be dipped in paint and touched quickly to a piece of paper to produce interesting strippled patterns. It is also used in the spattering technique described in chapter 4.

Be sure to clean your brushes thoroughly when you are finished with them. Use clear, running water on brushes that have been used with watercolor, poster paint, and acrylic colors. Turpentine is used to clean a brush used with oil paint.

Tape. Masking tape is a must for temporary placement of paper on paper and for holding stencils in place. Transparent *Scotch* tape is also useful; the double-sided tape can be used to hold paper together in place of glue.

Spatula. A spatula or palette knife is used to spread paint for screen printing and block prints. This can be done with a conventional putty knife, but it is somewhat unwieldy. Try a butterknife, if you have one.

Roller. A roller, or brayer, is used to spread paint on the raised surfaces of block prints.

Squeegee. A small window-cleaning squeegee is ideal for use with a silk screen printer. Pick one with a soft rubber blade.

Toothpicks. The simple little toothpick is one of the most helpful tools a cardmaker can have. It is used for applying wax to batik patterns, and gluing as well as for dabbing spots of color on designs.

Foil pans. You can buy these, or wait until the family has a meal that is frozen in one. Either way, these trays are a necessity for holding and mixing liquids. They are ideal for use with oil-based colors, which are difficult to remove from most surfaces. Just throw the pans away when you're finished with them.

Plate glass. A piece of flat glass can be held facing the sun or a bright light and used for tracing patterns—it is easy to see the pattern through your paper when it is held up to light this way. The glass is also a very useful surface on which to mix and spread paint for silk screen and linoleum block printing.

Styrofoam. Styrofoam is an ideal material for making block prints, as you will see when you read chapter 2. You can buy it in blocks at craft supply stores, salvage it from the bottom of supermarket meat trays, or get it from the packing used to ship fragile products.

Foil. Ordinary kitchen foil as well as paper-backed foil salvaged from commercial packaging is used in making several cards described in chapter 15.

Facial tissue. A facial tissue, such as Kleenex, is used for many things from wiping up spilled paint to cushioning foil as it is embossed. Have a good supply on hand all the time.

Self-adhering clear plastic. This is made under a number of trade names, but it is all about the same. It can be purchased in small sheets or bought by the yard, and is available at office supply stores, craft stores, and some variety stores. It is used to protect a picture and to hold a design to a card. Use it carefully. Once it touches paper, it's stuck—you don't get a second chance.

Burnisher. A burnisher is used to rub artist's transfer letters in place, and you might find it useful for smoothing other surfaces, too, such as two pieces of paper that have just been glued together, or for smoothing a self-adhesive plastic sheet onto the front of a card. Small, flat plastic wedges are sold as burnishers, and they work very well. Something like the back of a smooth spoon handle will work well, too.

Tweezers. When you have to handle and position tiny things, as you must when you work on some of the cards in this book, tweezers will come in very handy. Ordinary eyebrow tweezers will work very well.

Sewing machine. One of the cards we describe is made with a sewing machine. The card requires a zigzag attachment and an embroidery setting.

Iron. An ordinary clothes iron is used for many things in cardmaking. Everything from pressing the organdy for a silk screen to removing wax from batik and sealing pictures on a postcard can be done with an iron. Don't use a steam iron unless it can be used dry without damaging the iron.

Paints. There are a variety of paints for the cardmaker to choose from. Following is a description of some of the paints used on the cards in this book.

Acrylic paints are available in a wide assortment of vibrant colors. They can be lightened with white and will remain opaque, or they can be thinned with water to produce a watercolor effect. If you work quickly, you can even do a bit of sculpting of thick acrylic to produce a raised design which is not altogether unlike embossing. Acrylics dry quickly, so you must work fast. Always clean your brushes and other painting tools with clear water immediately after you use them with acrylic paint.

Poster paints are available in limited colors, but they are easy to use. For a wild effect, you can get these paints in fluorescent colors. Be sure to stir poster paint well before and while you're using it. The colors can be thinned with water, and water is used for cleaning.

Watercolors are used for subtle color. You can buy watercolors in pans or tubes, but the tubes are relatively expensive. Opaque white watercolor is needed for touch-up work on art that is to be given to a commercial printer.

Oil paints are recommended only for use with one card, the one produced by using oil and water (chapter 8). It is not really adaptable for other cards, and it takes forever to dry.

Aerosol color sprays can be used like an airbrush to create sprayed backgrounds and free-form designs on cards.

Inks. There are a number of different types of ink for the cardmaker. One ink, used mainly for block printing, is sold in tubes and behaves much like paint. This ink is water soluble. Liquid inks can be bought in a variety of brilliant colors, as well as in an intense black. Inks are best used when a transparent effect is desired. If you are planning to do your lettering with a waterproof ink instead of a pen marker, use a crow quill or a Speed Ball pen.

Food coloring and fabric dyes. Food coloring and textile dyes can be used effectively on paper and cloth. You can use these dyes to tint a photograph that is to be mounted on a card. Let the dyed photo dry between several sheets of weighted paper towels before mounting it.

Crayons. Seldom used for actual coloring on greeting cards, crayons have other uses for the cardmaker. For example, a white crayon can be used instead of melted wax when doing batik.

Paints, Inks, and Finishes

Turpentine. Use turpentine to thin oil colors and with the oil-water technique described in chapter 8.

Shellac. Shellac is used to prepare a silk screen design. It can be thinned with alcohol.

Wax. Used in making batik patterns, wax for cardmaking can be gathered from a number of sources: old candles, preserving paraffin, and birthday candles.

Clear plastic spray. A spray such as Krylon has many uses. It is ideal for protecting the surface of a sketch or a card and it can be used to preserve certain flowers.

Glues and Cements

White glue. Elmer's is one of the more popular white glues. It has some flexibility and can be used to join fabric to fabric, and yarn, string, and other items to paper. See individual card instructions for specific uses.

Rubber cement. When you want to join paper to paper or attach any of the other materials (other than fabric) used to make cards and avoid wrinkles, use rubber cement. If you spill rubber cement where it isn't wanted, wait until it dries before you try to lift it. Rub the dried cement with a "mouse" (a small ball of dried rubber cement) and it will lift right up. As you use your mouse it will get bigger and bigger with the cement it picks up. Rubber cement thickens quickly if the bottle is left open. But you can thin it out by mixing in a little rubber cement thinner. Add it a little at a time and stir vigorously until you have a nice useable consistency. *Caution:* rubber cement and its thinner are highly flammable. Never use it near a flame, and do not smoke while you have an open bottle.

Paper and Board

Carbon or transfer paper. Ordinary typing carbon paper can be used to transfer designs from one piece of paper to another, but the ink is greasy and difficult to erase. Rather than use carbon paper, we suggest that you make your own transfer paper. This is simply a piece of paper on which you have rubbed a soft pencil. Cover the entire sheet, and then wipe away the loose graphite with a facial tissue. There will be enough graphite left to handle any of the transfer jobs described in this book. And you will be able to erase the lines more easily than if you used carbon paper. White dressmaker's transfer paper is handy for transferring a design to dark paper. If none is available, you can make an effective white transfer sheet by covering a piece of tracing paper with white crayon. If you're not sure how to use transfer paper to duplicate a design, see How to Transfer a Design near the end of this chapter.

Tracing paper. This is needed for planning designs and making soft-pencil transfers. It can be bought in pads in art supply stores and some variety stores. If you can't get tracing paper, typing onion skin can be substituted.

Stencil paper. This is a heavy stock that is made specifically for cutting stencils. If none is available, you can substitute a heavy tracing vellum sheet.

Yellow typewriter paper. This is an inexpensive sheet that can be used for making rough sketches and doing experiments, and it is ideal for use as the silk screen stencil described in chapter 7.

Dry mount tissue. Sheets of this tissue are used to adhere a photo or other paper element to paper or card. It is applied with an electric iron.

Colored construction paper. This paper is relatively inexpensive and is ideal for use with block printing, pen marking, and all water-soluble paints. It is made in a wide range of colors.

Poster board. Poster board can be bought in many different colors. It is much stiffer than construction paper and is best used with marking pens or poster paint. It spots when it gets wet.

Colored art paper. These papers, used by professional artists, are available in a wide range of rich colors. The color is only on one side of the paper. However, they are relatively expensive. Seldom is it available anywhere but at art supply stores.

Bristol. A stiff paper that can be used for non-folded or single-fold cards, Bristol is too thick to use for cards that are folded in quarters (French fold). Bristol should be scored before it is folded, and rough edges can be repaired with a light rubbing of fine sandpaper. It takes all marking inks and paint well.

Typewriter paper. A good typewriter paper can be used to make the French fold cards described in this book. If you plan to do any printing or marking on typewriter paper, avoid the types that are advertised as being easily erased. These papers contain a compound that makes it difficult for the ink to take.

Colored stationery. It is possible to buy colored writing stationery and matching colored envelopes at some stationery stores. This paper is especially suited for silk screen and block printing.

Commercial paper. Perhaps the best source of unusual papers is your local printer. You (and he) cannot economically buy small enough quantities of these special papers, but often a printer will have enough trim scrap to keep you in business for quite a while. If the trim is still in a useable shape, the printer will probably charge you a nominal price for a few sheets. But if it is not useable on any of his presses, but still the right size for your cards, you should be able to cart away all you need without cost. Ask for English finishes; they are nice surfaces for the cardmaker to work with. The highly calendered (smooth) and coated glossy stocks are not very easy to use. An ordinary no. 1 sheet of 70 lb. offset stock is excellent and can be used with any of the inks, paints, and techniques described in this book. This paper is sold by many mills in a variety of colors, but you will have to take your chances when you hunt for scraps.

Etc., Etc., Etc.

Photos. Photographs and pictures printed in magazines can be used to make cards. See chapters 16 and 17 details.

Color transparencies. Large transparencies (slides) can be used directly in making cards, as described in chapter 18. However, any commercial photo lab can make blow-ups from your transparencies if they are too small to use as is.

Transfer letters. Used by commercial artists in their work, these letters can be used to create the lettering on your cards and will give your cards a professional look. Transfer letters are usually sold only in art supply stores.

Press-on plastic letters. Sold mainly in variety stores, these self-adhering letters are simply peeled off a backing and pressed in place.

Gold foil press-on letters. Made by Dennison, these letters add an impressive dimension to Valentines, congratulations, and similar cards. They are usually available in craft, stationery, and variety stores.

Linoleum. Buy linoleum ready blocked for block printing at a craft or art supply store, or get it in larger, unmounted sheets at a floor covering shop. Either way, the material is fun to work with, but be sure you get a set of linoleum chisels, too.

Thread and yarn. Colored cotton thread is used for the hand- and machine-stitched cards described in this book, and scraps of cord and yarn can be used to create abstract as well as representative designs (see chapter 19).

Linen and closely woven cotton. These materials have the body needed for hand-sewn designs.

Organdy. Organdy is the ideal inexpensive substitute for expensive silk when you make screen printings.

Things of nature. Sand, flowers, pebbles, seeds, leaves, and many other of nature's products can be used to make unusual cards. Many of the cards we describe use natural elements.

Envelopes

In chapter 24, we illustrate the different types of commercial envelopes which are readily available. However, your card idea may hinge on an off-size envelope. For those who would like to make their own, follow these instructions. Figure 1-1 shows dimensions for a standard size, but you can scale up or down very easily to suit your needs. This envelope is a baronial style, and it will accomodate most of the cards in this book.

To make the envelope, enlarge the pattern to suit your needs and then cut out your envelopes. Fold in the flaps in the lettered sequence, and glue flap C to flaps A and B.

Fig. 1-1 Pattern for homemade envelopes. Enlarge it to suit your needs.

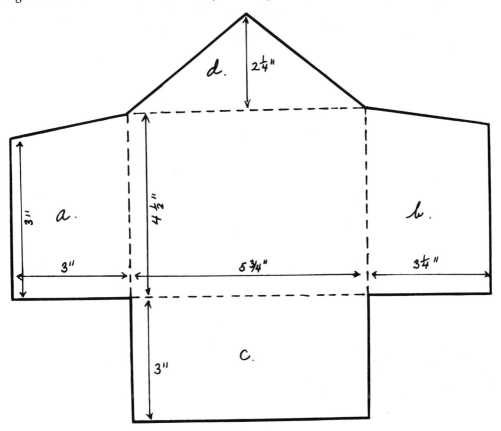

How to Transfer a Design

Once you have created a tracing paper sketch of your card or selected a pattern to use, it is usually necessary to transfer the design to the card paper or some other surface. This is easily done using carbon paper or homemade transfer paper (paper covered with soft pencil). Simply put the carbon or transfer paper face down on the card paper, put your tracing paper design on top, and, with a hard pencil, go over the outlines of the design. The lines will be transferred to the card paper. You should try to keep the lines as light as possible. If they are too dark, they may show on the completed card. If you have used homemade transfer paper, you can lighten the lines with an artgum eraser.

If you are transferring the design to a linoleum block or other surface which you will then be turning over to stamp or print the image, be sure to flop your tracing paper design before you transfer it. This means to turn the sketch over so you view it in reverse through the back of the tracing paper. When the reversed design is transferred and then the block is flopped to stamp or impress the image, the image will print correctly.

The French Fold

Many of the cards you will make will be based on the French fold. A French folded sheet is simply one which has been folded in quarters, once in each direction (see fig. 1-2). To get a smooth, tight fold, run a smooth tool, such as the handle of a spoon or the edge of a ruler, along the fold.

Now let's get on to making cards.

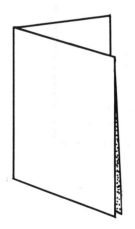

Fig. 1-2 A French fold.

Styrofoam Prints   2

How to use Styrofoam to print designs with varying textures

Styrofoam may seem a surprising material for the cardmaker to use. However, not only is it easy to work with (you carve your design in it, then brush it with paint, and stamp it on your card), but it comes in a variety of densities that will produce everything from bold, flat textures to delicate, lacy patterns. Smooth Styrofoam can be used to print impressions ranging from fine lines to a solid background for an entire card.

Best of all, it's possible to get just about all the Styrofoam you'll need for your cardmaking without ever spending a cent. The material is a very popular packaging plastic; everything from radios to glassware is packed in the airy Styrofoam blocks. And the meat you buy is most supermarkets is packaged in Styrofoam trays. The meat tray material is smooth and ideal for use in the bold, flat elements of a design.

Before you begin your design, it helps to print samples of all the Styrofoam textures you have been able to acquire. When you can see the printed textures, you will be better able to select the right ones to develop your design.

Styrofoam is the kind of material that lends itself to interesting experiments. For example, don't limit yourself to using only one impression—try overlapping two different textured blocks or printing different colors with the same block, but print the second color slightly off register with the first. Just plain flat prints of the same block, turned in a series of different positions and in different colors, can produce interesting patterns that will have a feeling of depth. As you tinker with this versatile material, you will discover many ways to use it.

Fig. 2-1 Christmas holly card, printed with two different textures of Styrofoam.

Fig. 2-2 Pattern for Christmas holly card.

Christmas Holly Card

Below are step-by-step directions for making a simple Styrofoam print card, like the one shown in fig. 2-1 (see also photo 1 in the color section). The card pictured is printed with two different textures of Styrofoam, but, of course, you can create your own design and use whatever textures you like—the technique is the same.

Materials

Styrofoam plastic. Use smooth-finish pieces from a food package to print solid areas and light-textured blocks from other packaging for lacy areas.
Paper on which to print the cards
No. 2 pencil (soft)
Tracing paper
Scissors
Carbon or transfer paper
Spoon handle or other blunt tool
Acrylic or poster paints
Small watercolor brush
Rubber cement or other glue
Heavy cardboard
X-acto knife

Directions

1. Select the size card you want, and cut enough paper for the number of cards you plan to make. Use colored paper if you like, but compare the paper with the paint you plan to use to make sure you have chosen colors that go well together. Cut about a half-dozen extra cards for your test prints.

2. Using either the pattern provided (fig. 2-2) or a design of your own, draw the card on tracing paper which has been ruled to the size card you want (fig. 2-3). We printed the holly sprig part of the pattern with smooth, untextured Styrofoam, and cut the star and a few other shapes from light-textured Styrofoam.

3. If you want to print a smooth-textured image with Styrofoam from a meat package, trim away the rim of the package so you will have a flat sheet with which to work. Select a flat, undented area of the smooth Styrofoam and cut it to the dimensions of the card you plan to make. You can use a mat knife or a razor blade, but a scissors will work just as well.

4. Turn the tracing paper over so that the design is now seen through the back in reverse. This is called flopping the image.

Place a piece of carbor paper or homemade transfer paper (see chapter 1) between the tracing paper and the Styrofoam, and trace the reversed image onto the plastic (fig. 2-4).

5. Now, using a pencil point, press down the background

Fig. 2-3 Draw the design on tracing paper.

Fig. 2-4 Transfer design to the Styrofoam.

Fig. 2-5 On smooth Styrofoam, press down around the design with a pencil.

Fig. 2-6 On lightly textured Styrofoam, cut away the background.

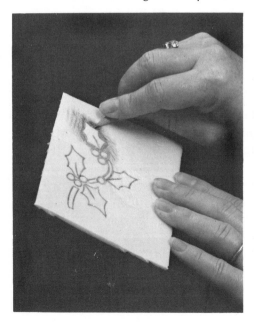

around the entire design. This will leave the design raised and it will stand out from the pencil-darkened area (fig. 2-5). Once the area around the design has been pressed down firmly with the pencil point, use a blunt tool such as a spoon handle to press down the rest of the background.

6. Paper patterns can be tacked to the lightly textured Styrofoam and cut out directly. When working with lightly textured Styrofoam, remove the background with an X-acto knife, rather than trying to press it down (fig. 2-6). If the image is to appear in a certain direction, be sure to flop the pattern before transfering it to the Styrofoam. Styrofoam is easy to cut, but be careful— trim away small pieces at a time to avoid damaging surfaces that will print (fig. 2-7). In figs. 2-7 through 2-9, the background has been darkened with poster paint so that the raised design can be seen clearly. It isn't necessary to do this when you make the card.

7. Cut a piece of heavy cardboard to the same size as the card. Trim away as much of the thin, smooth Styrofoam background as you can without weakening the material. Glue the Styrofoam to the cardboard in the position you want it to print. Remember, the image still appears in reverse. (fig. 2-8).

8. Apply the acrylic or poster paint to the image area with a brush (fig. 2-9). Try to avoid getting any paint on the background.

Fig. 2-7 Carefully cut away small pieces, so you don't damage the design.

Fig. 2-8 Cut away as much of the background as you can, and glue the Styrofoam to the cardboard.

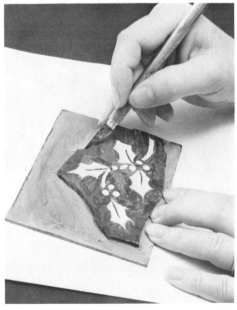

9. Position the block over the card, and press down evenly (fig. 2-10). Your first few printings should be considered tests—it may take several tries to get the coverage you want and to avoid making an uneven impression. Apply fresh paint to the block when the impression appears incomplete. We have found that it is wise to print on a flat sheet of paper, rather than on one which has been folded. The thickness of the folded edge can interfere with good printing. Save the folding until after the cards have all been printed and are dry.

10. If the card is to include additional impressions from other blocks either to complete the design with a different texture or to add another color, make sure that the impressions register with each other perfectly. Use some of your test prints from the first block to check for proper alignment.

More Tips for Styrofoam Prints

It may be necessary to touch up some of your first impressions with a brush, but once you get the feel of the block and the paints, you should be able to turn out perfect prints quite rapidly.

When using acrylic paint, squeeze out only a small amount at one time on a piece of clean cardboard. Poster paint should be stirred regularly as the printing proceeds. Do not use poster

Fig. 2-9 The paint can be applied to the raised design with a brush.

Fig. 2-10 Position the block on the card paper and press down firmly. (The paper here is larger than the block, for purposes of photographic contrast.)

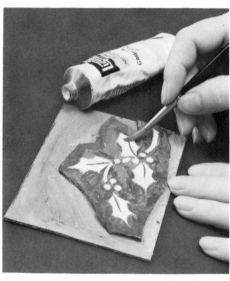

Fig. 2-11 More Styrofoam prints with various textures.

Fig. 2-12 Pattern for dandelion print.

paint too thin. You'll know when it's too thin—it will run and you will get fuzzy edges on your impressions.

If you notice that any of the texture is changing as you progress, it might be necessary to wipe the impression area of the block lightly with a damp paper towel.

If you plan to use the blocks again, wash off all of the paint and wrap them in paper towels for storage.

Figure 2-11 illustrates several designs which were created with Styrofoam blocks. (See also photo 1 in the color section.) The large sheet in the center demonstrates how designs can be created by using plastics of varying textures. You will find that it's best to cut highly detailed shapes like the dandelion leaves and petals in fig. 2-12 from smooth and relatively dense Styrofoam, whereas simpler shapes can be cut from either smooth or rough Styrofoam.

Linoleum Block Prints   3

How to carve linoleum and create prints with an old-world look

Virtually every culture has had some form of block printing—Oriental designers still use wood blocks to print elaborate patterns on fabric as well as on paper—but it wasn't until Americans started covering their wood floors with a substance called linoleum that amateur craftspeople revived the art here and added some new dimensions.

The fact that linoleum is inexpensive, has a smooth, even texture, and is easy to cut makes it an excellent material for the amateur as well as the professional. Many single- and multi-color cards that are sold in specialty shops are made by using linoleum blocks, and the technique is quite popular for making book plates.

When linoleum printing became popular, craft supply manufacturers decided to mount the material on wooden blocks, ready for cutting and printing. However, it's just as easy and a lot less expensive to use plain, ordinary battleship linoleum. Battleship linoleum is available in large sheets from floor covering dealers in ⅛″ and ¼″ thicknesses, or in smaller pieces from craft suppliers. This linoleum has a burlap backing.

Linoleum block printing is adaptable to most motifs, but it would be wise to avoid pictures in which perspective is important. Intricate scenes are difficult to create, and fussy lines will not reproduce very well. We have chosen a reindeer design to illustrate the technique.

Many block print designs look nice printed on a colored stock. But if you use construction paper, first soak the sheet in clear water for a half a minute and then let it dry between several sheets of heavy blotting paper. Weight the blotting paper down with several heavy books to keep the construction paper from curling as it dries (the drying will take at least a half hour). This process will enable the construction paper to take the ink better.

21

Fig. 3-1 Reindeer card—a linoleum block print.

Fig. 3-2 Pattern for reindeer card.

Our reindeer card (fig. 3-1; see also photo 2 in the color section) is made by first printing the design on colored paper, trimming the print down to size, and then gluing the print to a folded card.

Reindeer Card

Materials

Lineolum block
A set of linoleum cutting tools
Felt-tipped pen
Paper on which to sketch the design
Tracing paper
Pencil
White dressmaker's transfer paper if the linoleum is dark, or
    carbon paper if it is light
A piece of plate glass or ceramic tile
Water-soluble inks for block printing
Spatula or palette knife
Brayer (roller)
Non-coated paper on which to print the design
Paper for the base card
Rubber cement

Directions

1. Decide on the size of the card and get or cut a block of linoleum to that size. If you want to use a pre-blocked piece, check to see what sizes your local craft supply dealer has in stock, and work up your design accordingly. If you have bought a sheet of unmounted linoleum, it can be cut to size by first scoring the surface about $1/32''$ deep with an X-acto knife and then snapping the line across the edge of a table. The linoleum will break cleanly, but you will have to trim the burlap backing with a sharp knife.

2. Draw your design on a piece of paper. We've provided a pattern for the reindeer (fig. 3-2), if you'd like to use that design. Otherwise, create your own. When you've finished drawing it, ink in the areas that you want to print with the felt-tipped pen. The inked-in sketch will serve as a guide to the areas that will print when you tool the linoleum.

3. Make a tracing of the sketch. Flop the tracing (reverse it by turning it over) and transfer the design, as described in chapter 1, to the printing surface of the linoleum (fig. 3-3). If the lino-

leum is light, use carbon paper to transfer the design; on dark linoleum, use white dressmaker's transfer paper.

4. Remove the tracing paper and transfer paper. Using a fine, pointed tool, cut around the outline of the design (fig. 3-4). The cuts should be made so that the linoleum slopes down from the printing surface to the area that is being removed. Try not to have any undercuts (that is, cuts that dig underneath the surface that is to print), and avoid cutting straight down—you don't want the printing surface to be at a right angle with the supporting linoleum. The sloped cut will reduce the possibility of damage to the design edges.

5. Use the broader gouging tools to remove the larger areas that will not print (fig. 3-5).

6. After you have removed all the linoleum that is not part of the design, pour the water-soluble ink on the surface of a piece of clean glass or tile. Add a little water if the paint is too tacky. Use the spatula to spread the paint evenly, as wide as the brayer roller).

7. Roll the brayer in the water-soluble ink; be sure that the brayer surface is coated evenly (fig. 3-6).

8. Now roll the ink onto the block (fig. 3-7). Before you make a print, check to see if any part of the block is inked that shouldn't be. Remove any high spots from the background be-

Fig. 3-3 Transfer the design to the linoleum.

Fig. 3-4 Cut around the outline of the design with a fine cutting tool.

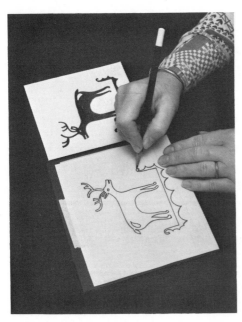

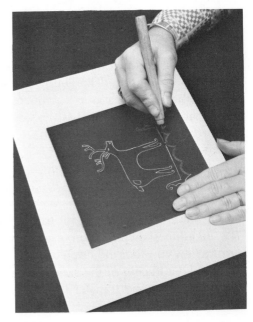

fore you go any further. Re-ink the block before each impression.

9. Press the block firmly on the card paper. A fair amount of pressure is required, but be careful in applying it so that you don't move the block once it is in position. (If you are using a fairly large piece of battleship linoleum, you might consider gluing it to a piece of wood before you begin printing. This will help ensure even printing and help prevent damage to the block.) To get the needed pressure you might try doing the printing on the floor and standing on the block. You can also use a mallet to give the block a few sharp raps. Be careful not to move the block when you tap it.

10. Cut the print to the size desired and mount it with rubber cement on a French-fold or single-fold card.

More Tips for Block Prints

Figure 3-8 (see also photo 2 in the color section) illustrates a card which was made by having the background as well as the design print.

On both the reindeer and candelabra prints, the ink was rolled on unevenly intentionally in order to provide a textural effect. It is just as easy to get a perfectly solid, smooth impression

Fig. 3-5 Remove the background with a wider cutting tool.

Fig. 3-6 Roll the brayer in the ink.

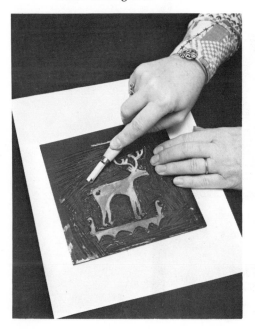

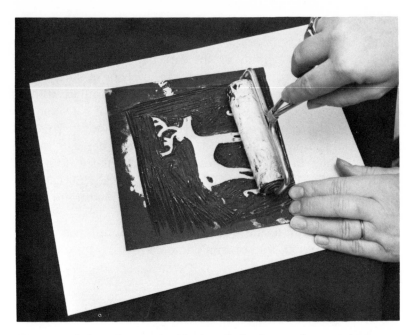

Fig. 3-7 Roll the ink onto the block and check to make sure there are no unwanted high spots getting inked.

Fig. 3-8 A different effect can be created by not removing all the background.

by spreading the ink carefully on the brayer and the surface of the block.

Linoleum is only one material that you can use to make cards. Actually any raised surface can be used to print a design, and some unique cards have been made by gluing string to heavy cardboard or by just fastening matches or toothpicks in a pattern. You might try carving an impression on a sliced raw potato, or producing a raised image on an ordinary gum eraser. Even leaves pasted on a piece of cardboard will produce a fine print if you are careful. What else can you think of?

4 Spattering

How to use paint spatters and stencils to produce subtle or bold effects

Spattering is a technique that can be used with many of the other cards we have described in this book. When you learn how to do it, you can produce everything from a light mist to bold patterns of paint droplets. And it's fun to do.

To create a spattered pattern, dip a stiff brush in ink or paint. Only the tips of the bristles should be dipped; excessive paint on the bristles will result in blobs, rather than a light, pleasing coverage.

Hold the brush in one hand with the bristles upright. Use a finger of the other hand to pull the bristles toward you and then let them snap forward to spray the paint on the paper. This technique can be used with a cut-out stencil, or to create free-form designs without a stencil. You can protect areas that are not to be spattered by covering them with masking tape and paper.

A stencil brush is ideal to use with this technique; it has stiff bristles and will snap the paint smartly as you pull them back with your finger. But, if a stencil brush is not at hand, try a toothbrush. Even soft toothbrush bristles will have enough snap for the job.

We have found that poster and acrylic paints seem to work best. But use them thick.

Before you try any cards, practice the technique to learn how much paint and pressure on the bristles will produce the patterns you want. After a little experimentation, you will get the feel for spattering and should have no trouble producing different textures.

Once you have become accustomed to spattering, you will be ready to try a card. You can make cards with spatter patterns alone, or you can use the technique to augment a basic design, such as we have illustrated with the skier (fig. 4-1). Turn to photo 4 in the insert to see this card in color. To make the card we

28

Fig. 4-1 Downhill skier card makes nice use of the spattering technique.

Fig. 4-2 Pattern for downhill skier card.

have created, follow the steps below. But if you have your own design ideas, use them in place of our material.

Downhill Skier Spatter Card

Materials

Stencil brush or toothbrush
Acrylic or poster paints
Tracing paper
Carbon or transfer paper
Colored paper
Stencil paper
X-acto knife
Paint brush
Pencil
Masking tape

Directions

1. Trace the line art shown in fig. 4-2 or create your own design on a piece of tracing paper (fig. 4-3).

2. Transfer the design very lightly, using carbon or transfer paper as described in chapter 1, onto a colored sheet of paper cut to size for your card. The line must be light, for you don't want it to show through the paint on the finished card.

3. Cut a mask (or stencil) out of the stencil paper (fig. 4-4),

Fig. 4-3 Draw your design on tracing paper.

Fig. 4-4 Cut a mask to block off portions you don't want covered with spatters.

and tape it in position over the colored paper. The mask is used to protect any part of your paper that you don't want covered with spattered paint. In our card, we first used the mask to block off an outline for the hill, but removed it before a second spattering which created the cloud of snow behind the skier.

4. Using the stencil brush dipped in white paint, spatter the paper to create the profile of the hill (fig. 4-5).

5. Remove the stencil and paint in the tree and the skier with white paint (fig. 4-6). Add shading to the skier with black paint to create dimension.

6. A final spatter is made just behind the skiing figure to add movement to the picture.

7. The spattered card can be made entirely of the colored paper, or the colored paper picture can be trimmed and mounted on a pre-folded white paper card, as we have done with this example.

In the downhill skier card, we limited the spattered color to white on a purple background. However, there is no reason to limit yourself to a single color design. Some very unusual non-objective motifs can be created using different color paints, by varying the size of the spatters, and by experimenting with placement and shape of your stencil.

More Tips for Spatter Cards

Fig. 4-5 Spatter paint over the exposed area of the paper.

Fig. 4-6 Paint in the other elements of the picture.

5 Marking Pen Needlepoint

How to create the quaint look of needlepoint with a few inexpensive markers

Some impressionist painters of the nineteenth century laid thousands of minute dots of pure color on their canvasses. As they developed their images, the impressions of the dots created beautifully and subtly colored pictures. But the color was not mixed on the artist's palate, it was mixed in the eye of the viewer—the dots blended visually to produce the hue that the artist desired.

With just a few of the color markers that are available today, you can use the same pointillist (from "points" or dots of color) technique to create a very realistic interpretation of a needlepoint pattern. The colors will not blend in the eye of the viewer, as did the colors of the impressionists, but the dots will make a very effective design.

Needlepoint patterns are not too easy to create, but there are enough pictures of these designs in modern magazines and catalogs so that most of your work will have been done for you. And, aside from modern designs, you can probably find reproductions of some of the famous patterns that were popular in a gentler era. Whether you use our design for a needlepoint bouquet in a basket (fig. 5-1, and photo 3 in the color insert) or come up with a design of your own, it is best to do your card on white paper, or a very light pastel, because you must be able to see through the paper to copy your design.

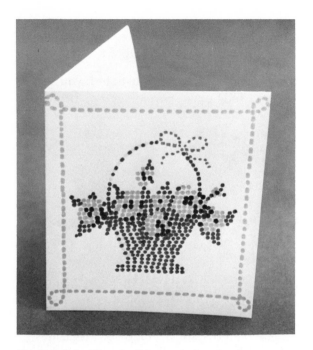

Fig. 5-1 "Needlepoint" bouquet in a basket.

Fig. 5-2 Pattern for the bouquet in a basket.

Bouquet in a Basket

Materials

Small-tipped marking pens. For the card illustrated, you will need these colors: red, pink, purple, green, brown, and yellow.
Drawing pencil
White paper for the cards
Tracing paper
Graph paper (³/₁₆″ squares)
Masking tape
Light table, a piece of plate glass, or a sunny window

Directions

1. Use the pattern in fig. 5-2, or find a needlepoint pattern that you want to use. It should be the size you want to reproduce; a larger pattern will have to be scaled down to fit the card. The best sources for these patterns are needlework magazines and catalogs.

2. Trace the pattern, outlining the colored areas (fig. 5-3).

3. Place the tracing paper over the sheet of graph paper and

Fig. 5-4 Put the tracing over graph paper and redraw the outlines of the design to give them a squared-off look.

Fig. 5-3 Trace the pattern you want to use.

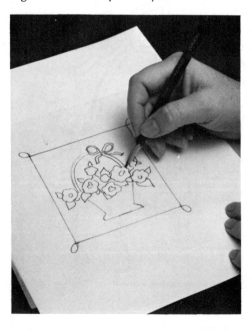

redraw all the outlines to give them a squarish look (fig. 5-4). It is this squared-up, right-angle look that will give your card the feeling of needlepoint.

4. Color each area of the design, using dots made with pens of the appropriate color (fig. 5-5). Try to keep all dots either at right angles to each other or else in horizontal rows. Also, each of the dots should be separated slightly by the white of the paper background. This, plus the attention to the right-angled look, will ensure that the final design resembles needlepoint. The completed needlepoint design on the tracing paper will serve as the pattern for your other cards.

5. For the next step, which is to copy the design onto the card paper, you will need either a light table, a piece of window glass, or access to a sunny window. We used a piece of glass placed next to a bright light. Tape the tracing paper pattern top and bottom to the glass, and then tape the unfolded card paper in the appropriate position over the pattern. Even with fairly heavy paper, you will still be able to distinguish the pattern and color of the needlepoint design.

6. Using the appropriate colors, reproduce the dots on the card (fig. 5-6). You can reproduce as many cards as you want this way.

Fig. 5-6 Tape the design to a sunny window or a piece of glass held up to a light, and then copy the design onto the card paper.

Fig. 5-5 Color the design with dots of various colored marking pens.

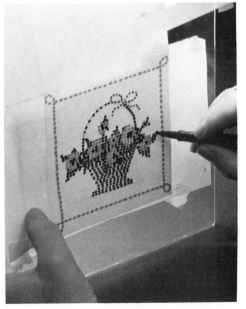

More Tips for Marking Pen Designs

Although this technique is great for imitating needlepoint, it is also ideal for anyone who would like to experiment. Building color and form by placing tiny dots of color on paper can be a rewarding experience. Everything from realistic images to very intriguing impressionistic pictures can be developed. To get an idea of what can be done with this technique, we suggest you try to see some of the paintings by Seurat and other pointillists, either in museums or reproduced in art books.

This technique can be used to produce cards on an unfolded sheet, or for single and French folds. However, if you plan to produce a folded card, make the dot reproductions with the paper unfolded; folded, you won't be able to see the pattern very well.

Marking pen needlepoint cards may appear to be very intricate and may seem difficult to make. However, once the master picture has been made, the reproductions can be turned out quickly and easily. And you should be able to make a hundred or more with one set of pens.

Batik   6

How to create intricate designs with an ancient, but simple, wax-resist technique

Batik, the process of selective dyeing, has changed very little since it was used to produce symbolic patterns by the Indonesians centuries ago. But with such modern conveniences as a stove and a few toothpicks, you can use the technique to make some very interesting cards.

Wax on the surface of cloth or paper prevents water from reaching the surface. If that water has dye in it, only those portions of the material which are not coated with wax will be dyed. The simplest of batik designs are made of a single color, but with careful planning, multi-color designs are easy to do, whether on cloth or paper.

Any motif can be used, but to take advantage of the technique, why not make your designs with an oriental feeling. Traditional batik has been influenced by Indian, Chinese, and Arabic decorative art. Free-form designs, such as the one we have used in the step-by-step project (fig. 6-1), were influenced mainly by Persian and Mexican traditions. Geometric patterns, like that shown in fig. 6-2, reflect the Indonesian influence. Both these cards are also pictured in the color section (photo 5).

You might want to try your hand at dyeing cloth to paste on a card, but the cards we have made here are of dyed paper. The process is essentially the same, though, whether you are using paper or cloth.

Fig. 6-1 Batik card with a free-form paisley design.

Fig. 6-2 Batik can also be used with a great effect on designs with a more geometric character.

Fig. 6-3 Pattern for batik paisley.

Fig. 6-4 Pattern for batik sun symbol.

Batik Card

Materials

Wax. The paraffin used in preserving, a melted white
candle, or an ordinary white children's crayon will do.
Uncoated white paper (typing paper is fine)
Soft pencil
Carbon or transfer paper
Blue and red construction paper
Small saucepan or double boiler
Toothpicks
Food color, fabric dye, or watercolor paint
Facial tissue
Shallow dish or pan
Rubber cement
An iron

Directions

1. Draw your own design, or use one of those pictured (figs.
6-3 and 6-4). Now transfer the design to the white paper with a
soft pencil, as described in chapter 1. Try to keep the lines as
light as possible.

2. Melt a small amount of wax in the saucepan over a low
flame. *Caution:* Wax is flammable. To reduce the fire hazard,
melt the wax in a double boiler.

3. Use the toothpick to apply melted wax to the design (fig.
6-5). Remember, wherever you put wax, the dye will *not* take. If
you want the design to be white, it should be covered so that
the background will be dyed. If the design is to be dyed, the
background should be covered with wax. If you have a large
area to cover, you might try using cotton on the end of the
toothpick, or a Q-tip.

4. Mix the food color, watercolor, or fabric dye with water in a
shallow pan (fig. 6-6). Some fabric dyes must be mixed with hot
water, so follow the manufacturer's instructions. You need
enough water to dip your paper or cloth into, and enough dye
mixed in to produce the color effect you want. Be sure that the
color is strong enough to produce sufficient contrast with the
rest of the design when the wax is removed. At this point, it is
wise to test the effect of the dye on scraps of waste paper or
cloth. When you think the color is right, proceed to the next
step.

5. Slide the waxed batik card into the dye and remove it
quickly to prevent the paper from curling (fig. 6-7). Blot the sur-

face of the card with clean facial tissue to remove excess dye from the surface.

6. Allow the card to dry naturally. If you try to dry it with a hair dryer or in an oven, there is a good chance that the card will curl.

7. When the card has dried completely, cover it with a piece of facial tissue and lightly iron it. The facial tissue will absorb the wax and leave the pattern you want.

8. The illustrated card was completed by fastening the batik design to blue and red construction paper. Use rubber cement for this. The blue piece is slightly smaller than the red to create a frame.

More Tips on Batiking

You can simplify the batik process by using an ordinary children's white crayon. Using this white crayon, there is no need to melt wax. All you have to do is go over the design with the crayon, as if you were coloring a picture. However, you should try to keep the point reasonably sharp if you are working with intricate designs. You can use your X-acto knife or some fine sandpaper to sharpen it.

It is possible to create multi-color cards using the batik process. Basically, it is a matter of repeating the process for each color, but it requires considerable attention to detail. And when a color is added over a color, the result is a third color. Multi-color batik requires considerable experimenting. Just be sure the paper is thoroughly dry before the next color is added.

Fig. 6-5 Apply the melted wax to the design with a toothpick.

Fig. 6-6 Mix the dye with water in a pan.

Fig. 6-7 Submerge the waxed design in the dye, and remove it promptly.

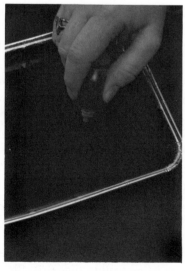

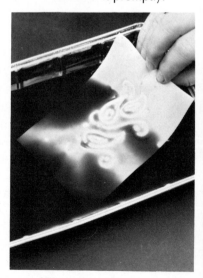

Silk Screen   7

*How to make screen prints
for either large runs or
special editions*

In many ways, the silk screen process bears a considerable resemblance to its oriental ancestor, the stencil. But, today, artists who produce serious work (serigraphs) with the silk screen have refined the technique to a state in which subtle gradations of tone and fine lines, as well as bold shapes and colors, are possible. The work of many fine printmakers is included in permanent museum collections all over the world.

For the cardmaker, the silk screen represents an opportunity to do fine artistic work as well as to produce cards in sufficient quantities so they can be sold profitably. The screens we describe in this chapter can be used to produce up to one hundred cards, but are not durable enough to make many more. However, the technique is basically the same as that used in commercial printing. To be used for long runs, screens are prepared and mounted on wooden frames. These frames help speed up the process and allow for more accurate work.

When a simple stencil is used to print a design, a cut-out is made of stencil paper, the stencil is placed against the surface on which it is to be printed, and paint is applied to the exposed area with a stencil brush. However, in the silk screen process, the area that is to print is covered with a piece of tightly stretched silk, or a similar fabric. When the paint is drawn across the screen stencil with a squeegee, it is forced through the openings between the fabric threads. The screen controls the amount of ink that will be deposited on the paper. The silk screen process is faster than stenciling, and the result is more uniform coverage.

The first screen printing technique takes you one step past the basic stencil: a screen is made by positioning a paper stencil on a piece of organdy. The second technique will bring you closer to the contemporary methods of screen printing: the screen is blocked with shellac, allowing only the open areas to print.

Fig. 7-1 Silk screen prancing cat.

Fig. 7-2 Pattern for prancing cat.

This card (fig. 7-1 and color photo 8) uses a screen made with a paper stencil and a piece of organdy. The print is made directly on the card paper, which can be any uncoated (non-glossy) paper or construction paper.

Prancing Cat Card
Paper Stencil Method

Materials

Paper for the stencil. Inexpensive yellow typewriter paper will do very well
Pencil
Tracing paper
Carbon or transfer paper
Scrap paper
Organdy
Masking tape
Manicure scissors or small sewing scissors
Rubber cement
Heavy cardboard for the card frame. The back of a tracing pad is ideal.
Heavy white paper for card position guide
Uncoated paper or construction paper on which to print the cards
Spatula or palette knife
Small window-cleaning squeegee
Black marking pen
Acrylic or thick poster paint
Iron

Directions

1. Make a tracing of the cat design (fig. 7-2), or create your own motif. To create your own design for this basic silk screen, bold shapes are best. Fine detail can be printed by silk screen, but more sophisticated equipment is needed. In addition to the outline of the cat's body, the eyes and the inside of the ears are glued down separately. The head and the body are separate, with the paper background forming the collar.

2. Flop the tracing paper design and transfer it to the stencil paper (fig. 7-3). You can do this with carbon paper or transfer paper, as described in chapter 1.

3. Cut out the stencil with the manicure scissors (fig. 7-4). *Don't* make a cut from the edge of the paper into the cat—just cut around the outlines of the design.

4. Use the iron to press the organdy so that it is absolutely flat.

5. Glue the entire stencil to the organdy with rubber cement, and glue down any details within the cut-out area where you don't want the paint to print (the cat's ears and eyes, for example). Be sure that no cement adheres to any part of the design that will be used to print.

6. Make a card position guide for the screen by cutting out a shape the same size as the front of your card from the heavy white paper. Single cards made of light paper can be positioned and printed directly. However, if you plan to make a folded card of fairly heavy paper, it should be printed before it's folded. Make the guide to position that portion of the unfolded card that will be printed. Tape the guide to the piece of heavy cardboard. The cut-out will serve to position the card during the printing process.

7. Position the screen stencil over the card position guide so the design falls where it is to print. The paper stencil should face down and contact the paper to be printed. Tape the screen stencil at one end, and fold it back at the tape joint to make a workable hinge (fig. 7-5).

8. Cut your card paper to size, position a card in the cut-out

Fig. 7-3 Flop the design and transfer it to stencil paper.

Fig. 7-4 Carefully cut out the design from the stencil paper.

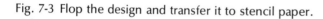

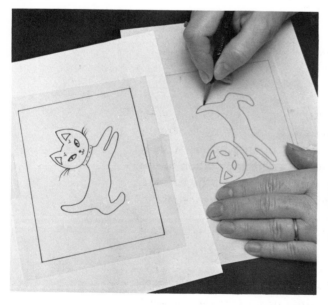

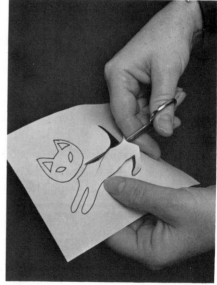

on the piece of cardboard, and gently tape the card in place. Put the screen over the card and smooth it down.

9. Squeeze out a little paint along the top of the screen, at the masking tape hinge. Use the spatula or palette knife to spread the paint evenly across the top, preparing it to be drawn down across the stencil with the squeegee.

10. Use the squeegee to draw the paint down across the surface of the screen. In fig. 7-6 we have positioned the squeegee so that the paint is visible. This is *not* the correct position for printing. The handle should be down, and the blade should be angled so its bottom edge faces away from you as you pull the squeegee. Once you start the squeegee in motion, continue at a steady rate until you reach the end of the screen.

11. Lift the stencil and examine the print (fig. 7-7). If it's uneven, too heavy, or too light, experiment with different amounts of pressure on the squeegee until you get what you want. You might have to make several test prints before you get the impression you want. It's a matter of getting a feeling for the pressure and the stroke. Once you have a print the way you want it, repeat the approach for succeeding cards.

Fig. 7-5 Position the screen over the frame, and tape down one end of it so the screen can be folded back.

Fig. 7-6 The squeegee is being held up (*not* in position for printing!) so you can see the paint spread across the top edge of the screen.

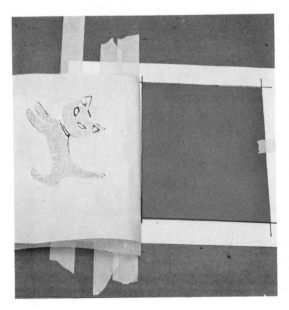

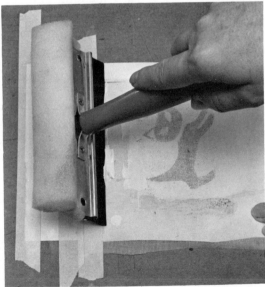

Fig. 7-7 Lift up the screen and see what you've got.

12. Before you start the next card, the paint must be scraped back to the top of the stencil. Use the squeegee to do this, but place a piece of scrap paper under the stencil first. When the paint runs low, replace it (see step 10).

13. You might want to add a few simple embellishments with a marking pen, as was done to our cat card. Whiskers, eyebrows, a nose, eye pupils, and a collar were added for finishing touches with a black fine point marker.

Pennsylvania Dutch Valentine
Shellac Resist Method

Our Pennsylvania Dutch Valentine (fig. 7-8 and color photo 8) is printed with a shellac resist screen on a square of paper, which is then mounted on a folded card. Of course, you can print directly onto your card too.

Materials

Fine point marking pen
Organdy
Masking tape
Shellac
Small brush
Thinner (alcohol)
Heavy white paper
Heavy cardboard

Uncoated paper or construction paper on which to print the
    design
Paper for the base card
Small window-cleaning squeegee
Acrylic or thick poster paint
Spatula or palette knife
Rubber cement
Iron

Directions

1. Press the organdy. Be sure that it is flat and that there are no traces of a fold.

2. Trace the design (use the one in fig. 7-9 or create one of your own) onto the organdy with a fine point marking pen (fig. 7-10).

3. Put strips of masking tape on all four sides of the organdy. This will make it easier to work with the fabric.

4. Use the brush to apply slightly thinned shellac wherever the design in *not* to print (fig. 7-11). If you hold the organdy at an angle to the light, you will be able to see all of the uncoated spots more easily. After you have applied the shellac to the non-printing areas, hold the screen up to a light and look for un-coated spots. Fill these holes with shellac. Every pin hole must be covered.

Fig. 7-8 Pennsylvania Dutch Valentine.

Fig. 7-9 Pattern for Valentine.

5. Prepare a printing guide frame out of the heavy white paper and cardboard as described in step 6 of the prancing cat card. Put the dried shellac resist screen in place over the frame, and tape it securely in position *at one end* (fig. 7-12).

6. Cut the paper you are going to print on to shape, and position a piece in the cut-out in the frame. Lower the screen in position for printing.

7. Squeeze paint across the top of the screen on the masking tape hinge. Spread the paint evenly with the spatula so that it can be drawn evenly down the screen with the squeegee.

8. Draw the paint with the squeegee down across the surface of the screen. Do this firmly and with a steady movement.

9. Lift the screen and examine the first print. If it is uneven, too heavy, or too light, experiment with different squeegee pressures until you have what you want.

10. Before you print the second card, scrape the paint back to the top of the screen with the squeegee. Put a piece of scrap paper under the screen as you do so. Add more paint, if necessary.

11. If you haven't printed on the card directly, mount the silk screen print on a single- or French-fold card with rubber cement.

Fig. 7-10 Trace the pattern onto the organdy with a fine-tipped marking pen.

Fig. 7-11 Paint shellac over the areas that are *not* to print.

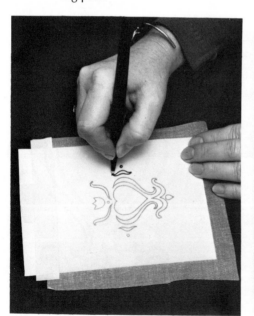

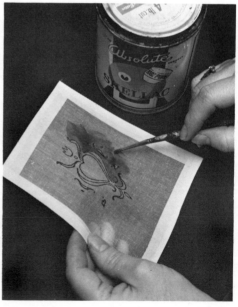

Fig. 7-12 Tape the screen in place over the
frame.

More Tips on Silk Screening

Whichever process you use (paper stencil or shellac resist), when you get the hang of it you will be able to turn out quite a few cards at one time. Remember to clean the stencil with fresh water after you have finished. The screens can be used again and again if they are cared for properly.

When you get adventurous, you can try printing more than one color on a single card. Figure 7-13 (see also color photo 8) shows a Christmas wreath that was printed in two colors. Each color uses a separate screen. We have included the patterns for each screen (figs. 7-14 and 7-15) in case you'd like to try this design. Figure 7-16 shows how the two patterns fit together.

Two-color printing is done in separate runs; be sure the first color has dried before you print the second. The second impression must be positioned carefully so that it registers with the first impression. To make sure that you end up with all the cards you want, print more than you need of the first impression. You will need the extras to make test prints of the second impression to ensure proper registration. (Of course, slight imperfections in registration are part of the character of silk screen prints.)

Silk screen is an ideal technique to use in making notepaper. Once you are set up, you can run off a quantity that will last quite a while.

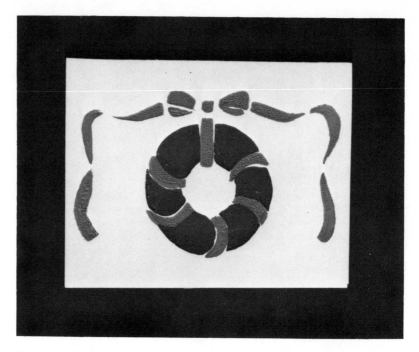

Fig. 7-13 Christmas wreath—a silk screen card in two colors.

Fig. 7-14 Pattern for the first color.

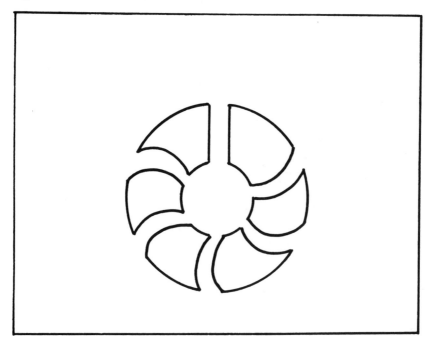

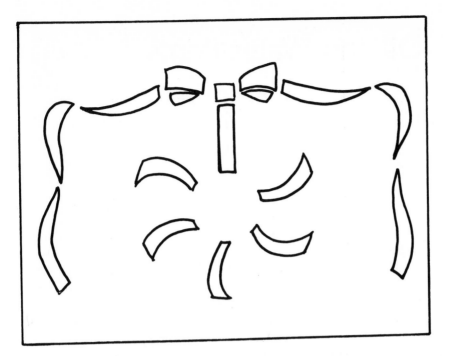

Fig. 7-15 Pattern for the second color.

Fig. 7-16 The two patterns together.

8 Oil and Water Prints

How to mix oil paint and water to produce beautiful, one-of-a-kind patterns

The patterns you can make with a swirl of oil paint in water are endless, and you'll never have two alike. This technique can be used to produce unusual backgrounds for cards, or shapes cut out of the patterned paper can become the decorative elements on a plain-background card. (This same oil and water process is used to create fancy endpapers in books.) It's a versatile technique that can be fun to use, just to watch the patterns develop.

We have used the oil and water prints in combination with other papers to create the card design, and have made an unusual picture frame card, too (fig. 8-1). If you want to expand the design possibilities, you could use other techniques such as a silk screen or block print, to print over paper that has been prepared with a subtle oil and water pattern.

Fig. 8-1 Cards with oil and water prints.

Basic Oil and Water Prints

Materials

Tube of oil paint
Turpentine
Water
Disposable foil pans
Brush
Uncoated paper. Plain white typing paper or light-colored construction paper is ideal.

Directions

1. Squeeze a small amount of the oil paint into a pan. Dilute the paint with turpentine until the color is runny. Make sure the mixing is complete (fig. 8-2).

2. Pour enough water into another pan to half fill it.

3. Pour the oil color and turpentine mixture into the pan with the water (fig. 8-3).

4. Swirl the mixture with the brush and wait until a pattern you like appears (fig. 8-4).

5. Dip the paper in at the end of the tray, putting it under the

Fig. 8-2 Thoroughly mix the oil paint with enough turpentine to make it runny.

Fig. 8-3 Pour the oil paint and turpentine mixture into a pan of water.

floating oil pattern. slowly lift the paper out through the oil. Watch the pattern develop (fig. 8-5). As long as there is enough oil color, you can continue to produce patterns. When the patterns become sparse, add more of the oil and turpentine mixture.

6. Dry the prints for several days in the open air. Put them face up on pieces of newspaper and let them dry in a place where there is little dust in the air.

7. Use the finished sheets as the background for designs, or cut them into patterns to be mounted on cards, as shown on the left and right in fig. 8-1. To make a picture frame as shown in the center of fig 8-1, follow the pattern (fig. 8-6), adjusting the size to suit your needs.

More Tips for Oil and Water Prints

In the examples we have used to illustrate this chapter, only one color of paint was used. However, you can use the same technique to produce multi-colored oil and water patterns. The safest way to do this is to print one color at a time, each color in a separate pan of water. Let one pattern dry before the next is applied. The more experimental of our readers might want to try swirling several colors in the water at one time. You can get some very beautiful patterns, but before too long the thinned oil colors will blend and you will be left with a single color. But you will have a lot of fun and produce some interesting multi-colored patterns.

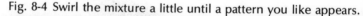

Fig. 8-4 Swirl the mixture a little until a pattern you like appears.

1 Styrofoam block prints, using several textures of Styrofoam.

2 Linoleum block prints, with the appealing folk-art look that characterizes the technique.

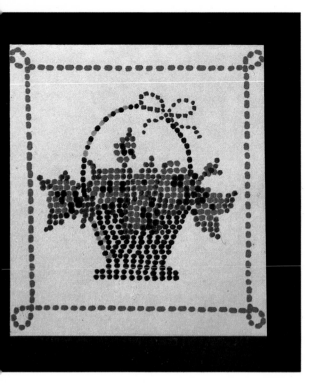

3 A traditional needlepoint design, quickly executed with colored marking pens.

4 A soft, spattered background setting off hand-painted details—one way to use spatters.

5 Batik cards. Sun design using food- or watercolor over crayon (left) and paisley pattern using trailed-on melted wax (right).

6 Tissue paper landscape utilizing the translucence of the thin paper to build up and give depth to the color areas.

7 Tissue paper cards. From left to right: folded paper roses; quilled miniature rosebush; Styrofoam print on tissue paper background.

8 Silk screen prints. From left to right: two-color Christmas wreath; Pennsylvania Dutch Valentine; prancing cat.

9 Paper mosaic rooster—a colorful mix of construction paper and confetti.

10 Three-dimensional pop-ups. From left to right: flower petal pop-up; sandy beach card; window-on-the-garden card.

11 Paper silhouettes—a way to show off simple as well as more intricate designs.

12 A pop-up Christmas card cheerfully doubling as a tree ornament.

13 More paper mosaics. From left to right: floral pattern of confetti; abstract design with cut paper; Christmas tree of self-adhesive office labels.

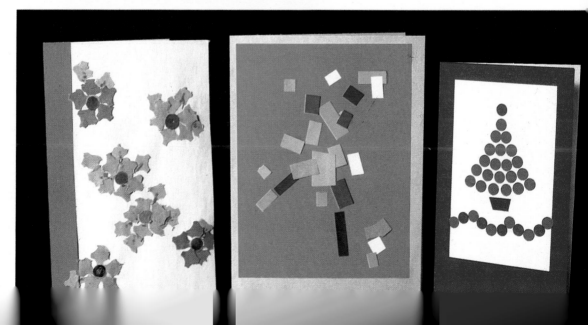

14 Decoupage Easter card, using pieces of rickrack and colored paper.

15 Another decoupage design, with colorful fabric scraps glued to a paper background.

16 Chinese tangrams—puzzle pieces to arrange in pictures or in abstract patterns.

17 Decoupage
Valentines and an-
niversary card, with
doilies, decals, gold
stickers, and
colored papers.

18 Commercially
printed black and
white line art (left),
hand-tinted with
watercolor (right).

19 String and yarn
cards. Geometric
string design with
paper cut-out (left)
and flowing abstract
yarn painting (right).

20 Sewn cards. From left to right: machine-embroidered Christmas tree; hand-stitched desert landscape on linen; cloverleaf and blossoms hand-stitched on felt.

21 Seeds, dried flowers, sand, and other materials add natural beauty to personal greetings.

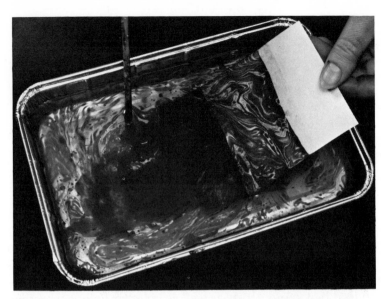

Fig. 8-5 Dip the paper underneath the swirls and gently lift it out
through the oil.

Fig. 8-6 Pattern for picture frame. Cut along the heavy lines and fold back along
the dotted lines.

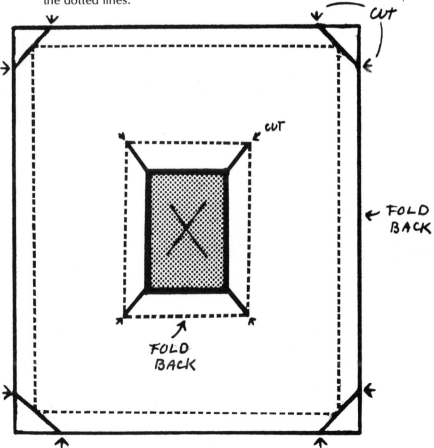

9 Silhouettes

How to make simple but striking paper cut-outs

In the era that predated the camera, one of the most popular ways of producing a personal likeness was the silhouette, and George Washington was probably the most silhouetted American. Also called shadowgraphs or profiles, these likenesses were produced by famous artists as well as itinerant tinkers who traveled the American countryside. Today, these silhouettes are showing up as antiques and collectibles and have set the stage for a revival of an art that can be applied to greeting cards very nicely.

Unless you are particularly skilled at cutting a picture with no lines to follow, we suggest that you first make a sketch on the back of the silhouette paper. There is a dense black paper that is made for this art, but if you are unable to get it, any stiff, snappy paper will do. A floppy paper will be particularly difficult to work with. You can also try making your own silhouette paper. Brush a coat of India ink on a piece of good bond typing paper, and you will have what is needed.

Fig. 9-1 Silhouetted rosebud
greeting card.

Fig. 9-2 Pattern for rosebud and ribbon silhouettes.

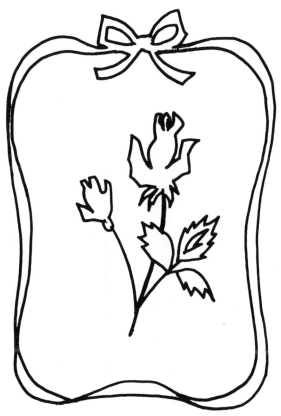

Rosebud Greeting Card
Solid Silhouette

One way to make a silhouette is to cut out the image in a solid shape, as shown in the cards in figs. 9-1 and 9-3 (see also color photo 11). Note in fig. 9-3 that all parts of the cut-out designs are connected to each other—the silhouette is all one piece.

Materials

Nail or cuticle scissors
X-acto knife
Tracing paper
Pencil
Carbon or transfer paper
Silhouette paper or any paper with some stiffness
Paper on which to mount the silhouette
Rubber cement

Directions

1. Select a design whose parts touch each other at many points. The designs we have shown meet this requirement.

2. Copy the design on tracing paper. You might want to use our pattern for the rosebud and ribbon (fig. 9-2).

3. Transfer the design to the *back* of the silhouette paper with carbon paper or transfer paper, as described in chapter 1. Before you transfer the design, flop (turn over) the tracing. The image on the back of the silhouette paper will now be opposite to the

Fig. 9-3 Other examples of silhouettes cut in solid shapes. Note that each silhouette is in one piece.

Fig. 9-4 Transfer the pattern to the back of
the silhouette paper and carefully
cut it out.

original. But when the silhouette is finished and turned over, it
will be positioned correctly.

4. Make the major cuts with the small scissors (fig. 9-4).
Where there are tight cuts and small openings to be made, such
as the highlight in the center leaf of the rosebud silhouette, use
the X-acto knife.

5. Handle the completed silhouette gently. Apply rubber cement to the back of the shape and mount it on the face of the
card. Any excess rubber cement should be allowed to dry and
then rubbed away very carefully. It's very easy to lift and tear
fragile portions of the silhouette.

The rosebud card was made by silhouetting an entire image. The
outline type silhouette, illustrated in fig. 9-5, can be fun to
make, too. Again, choose a design which has many points of
contact and few loosely attached pieces. Follow the instructions
for transferring the pattern, cutting the silhouette, and gluing it
in place as described for the rosebud greeting card.

However, it might be advisable to cut all of this silhouette with
an X-acto knife (fig. 9-7). When you get down to the thin strips,

Nativity Scene
Outline
Silhouette

Fig. 9-5 Nativity scene—an outline silhouette.

Fig. 9-6 Pattern for Nativity scene.

there is a chance of ripping. You can reduce this possibility by making sure that the blade is new, sharp, and has no nicks. Make your cuts slowly. If you feel the paper pulling as you cut, stop and hold it closer to the point at which you are cutting and proceed very slowly.

If you use a thin silhouette paper, you should be able to cut three at a time—carefully! (Early silhouette artists often lightly glued several pieces of paper together and cut a number of silhouettes at once. You can do the same. Be sure to apply the glue *outside* the image area of the silhouette.) And, once you sharpen you cutting skill, it will take no time at all to mount the finished patterns. Although the silhouette card gives the impression of being intricate and time-consuming, with a little practice you should be able to turn them out rather quickly.

Materials other than paper can be used for silhouettes. For example, heavy colored artists acetate can be very effective. It is usually impossible to trace a design onto this material, but you can attach the traced paper design with rubber cement. After the silhouette has been cut, just peel away the paper. But do this very carefully. Rather than mount the acetate silhouette on paper, think about using either clear or another color acetate as the base of the card. Such a silhouette could be mounted for display in a sunlit window, as we have described in chapter 18.

More Tips on Silhouettes

Fig. 9-7 Outline silhouettes are best cut
   with an X-acto knife.

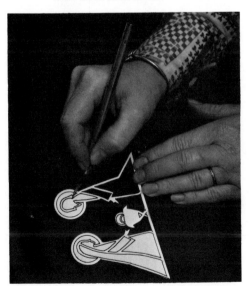

10   Paper Mosaics

How to create colorful, fanciful designs with bits of paper and confetti

Confetti, the little scraps of paper people throw at weddings and New Year's Eve parties, can be used to make some very interesting cards. Your designs can be carefully assembled by using different shapes and colors of confetti, or you can have a lot of fun making random designs with some glue and paper.

Some designs are made with just a single layer of confetti, but others can be given a three-dimensional look by building layer upon layer. The little rooster we used to illustrate this technique (fig. 10-1; see also color photo 9) was layered to give the impression of plumpness one often associates with barnyard birds. The confetti pieces were positioned at the neck and head in a flat plane, but as the body expands toward the tail, more paper scraps were added on top of each other to produce a chubby bird.

In addition to confetti, the rooster card uses some simple cutouts to help produce the image of the bird. This could have been done with ink or paint, but in this case the cut-outs contribute to the feeling of depth. Placing the rooster on a fence that leads out of the picture further enhances the three-dimensional quality.

You can make your own confetti with sheets of colored paper, scissors, and a paper punch. But if you can get it, we suggest buying bags of ready-made confetti. Not only will you get pieces of round punched paper, you will also get a marvelous assortment of different shapes that can be used to enhance the texture of your cards.

If you can put up with the mess, making confetti cards is a wonderful way to entertain children while you are helping them understand design, color, and composition.

Fig. 10-1 Paper mosaic rooster.

Fig. 10-2 Pattern for rooster.

Mosaic Rooster Card

Materials

A bag of multi-color, ready-made confetti or a supply of homemade confetti

Tracing paper

Pencil

Carbon paper

Paper for the card

Colored construction paper for other parts of the design

Tweezers

White glue

Scissors

Directions

1. Cut the card paper for the size card you plan to make.

2. Next draw an original picture, copy someone else's design, or use our pattern for the rooster (fig. 10-2). Make a sketch of your design on tracing paper (fig. 10-3).

3. Once you have completed the sketch on the tracing paper, use the carbon paper to transfer it, as described in chapter 1, to a piece of white paper. Also make a very light tracing on the paper that will be used for the card.

Fig. 10-3 Draw your design on tracing paper.

Fig. 10-4 Arrange the confetti on the design before gluing it on the card.

4. Make a trial arrangement of the confetti on the white paper. Arrange for color and shape (fig. 10-4). Once you have a pattern that pleases you, you can use it as a model when you glue down the confetti on the card paper.

5. Cut out and glue down the parts that will be covered with confetti first, such as the rooster's tail.

6. To paste down the confetti, lightly smear white glue over the area to be covered and position the paper bits. If you are planning to layer confetti on confetti to add depth to the picture, use the glue sparingly on the succeeding layers. Even though it dries transparent, any visible surface with glue on it will have a slight sheen that can detract from the overall effect.

7. Glue down remaining design pieces and add details, if you wish, with marking pens.

More Tips on Paper Mosaics

Figure 10-5 illustrates some other designs made with confetti. These can also be seen in color photo 13.

For some mosaic designs, you might try using self-adhesive colored dots made by Avery Label Products. They can be bought in most stationery or variety stores. The Christmas tree in fig. 10-5 was made entirely from these self-adhering dots, except for the little cut-out of the tub. The card in the center is based

Fig. 10-5 More paper mosaics.

on a floral design. The card at the right was made with hand-cut pieces of colored paper, arranged to produce an interesting nonobjective motif.

Don't stop here! Think of all the things you can do with confetti. In addition to making cards entirely with it, you can also use confetti to dress up cards made with other techniques. Just a touch of confetti on many of the cards described in this book will add interest and dimension.

You can also use confetti to spell out the greeting. First, hand-letter the message, then lightly spread glue on the letters and paste down the confetti.

Paper Weaving

How to weave a card with strips of paper, or ribbon, or fabric, or . . .

No loom is needed to weave this card (fig. 11-1). We have used a basketweave pattern, which is an obvious application of the technique, but an imaginative cardmaker can create tartan patterns for a Scottish friend, or make a wide variety of geometric designs simply by varying the color and width of the strips of paper.

The weaver can be subtle with color, or the card can have the vibrant flair of a fiesta. This is one project where you can experiment with different colors and produce designs that are uniquely yours without having to spend endless hours mixing

Fig. 11-1 Woven basket card.

Fig. 11-2 Weave the yellow strips over and under the brown strips.

Fig. 11-3 Pattern for basket cut-out.

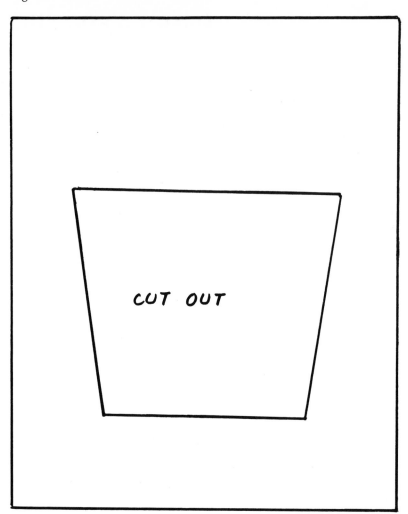

Fig. 11-4 Pattern for greenery.

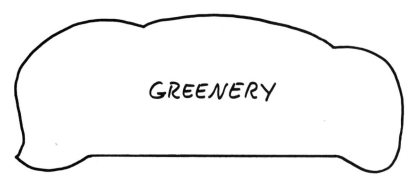

and matching paint. Just weave a few strips of paper together and see if you like the result. If you want to change the design, separate the strips and try other colors. You don't have to be able to visualize the end result—you can have it in a few seconds.

Materials

Woven
Basket
Card

Scissors
X-acto knife
Masking tape
Straight edge
Rubber cement
Pencil
Tracing paper
Colored construction paper (green, blue, yellow, brown, and pink)
Transfer paper
White Bristol paper
White typing paper

Fig. 11-5 Pattern for flowers.

Directions

1. Cut out seven strips of yellow and six strips of brown construction paper, all ½" x 3½".

2. Cut a piece of white typing paper 4¼" x 5" and position the strips of brown paper vertically, side-by-side, and just touching each other on the paper. To insure perfect alignment of the paper strips, you can draw a line across the white paper, about 1" from the top. Tape down the top edges of the brown paper strips to the white paper, using the line as a guide.

3. Put a yellow strip over the top of the left-hand brown strip, then under the next brown strip, and so on until it has been fully woven across all the brown strips.

4. Cut a piece of masking tape about 4" long and attach it beyond the left-hand corner of the taped-down brown strips. Keep the tape out of the way as each yellow strip is woven, but upon weaving each strip, bring the tape down far enough to hold the strip in place.

5. Weave a second yellow strip, but begin by placing it under the first brown one, over the second, etc., until the strip has been fully woven across all of the brown strips. Repeat this process with all of the yellow strips. Adjust the strips so they fit snugly and there are no spaces between them (fig. 11-2).

6. Use the scissors to trim the loose ends of the strips on the botton and right side; leave about ¼" for taping. Use masking tape to secure the remaining sides of the woven pattern to the white paper.

7. Copy the pattern of the basket cut-out (fig. 11-3) on tracing paper and transfer it, as described in chapter 1, to the blue construction paper. Use an X-acto knife and a straight edge to cut out the basket shape.

8. Position the woven design behind the basket cut-out and use rubber cement to join the two elements together (fig. 11-6).

9. Trace the greenery pattern (fig. 11-4) and transfer it to the green construction paper. Cut out this background and cement it above the top of the basket. The flat portion of the greenery should match the top of the basket cut-out.

10. The flowers are shown in fig. 11-5. This pattern not only provides the shapes of the flowers, it also shows how they are to be positioned on the greenery background. Each flower is cut separately from pink construction paper. The larger inner circles of the flowers are made of yellow paper and the center dots are

green. Copy each pattern on tracing paper, transfer them to the appropriate color construction paper, and cut them out.

11. Cement the flowers onto the greenery, overlapping them as shown in fig. 11-5. Then glue down the larger yellow centers and then the smaller green dots on each flower.

12. Cut a piece of white Bristol paper to 5$\frac{1}{8}$" x 8$\frac{1}{4}$" and make a single-fold card. Rubber cement the completed design to the front of the folded Bristol paper. Make sure that the left side of the blue background is flush with the fold on the left. Trim away the top of the card, as shown in fig. 11-7.

Figure 11-8 illustrates a woven design in which color and strip width were varied to provide interest. Figure 11-9 shows how a strip of paper can be woven into a sheet of paper to create a pattern. Slits were cut in the lower portion of the paper with an X-acto knife to permit the weaving. The fringe was made by cutting a series of slits in a piece of paper at even intervals. The uncut portion of the fringe was glued to the back of the card. The star

More Tips for Woven Cards

Fig. 11-6 Put the basketweave behind the basket cut-out and glue the two together.

Fig. 11-7 Neatly trim the top of the card to the shape of the flowers and greenery.

was cut as two triangles. One triangle was slit to permit the intertwining of the sides of the star.

Paper is not the only material that can be used to weave a card. Colored plastic such as that used to wrap holiday packages, ribbons, pieces of cloth, and even some of the colored decorative tapes can be adapted. You might even try dying string different colors and weaving it in the same fashion. Very thin wood shavings, such as those made when wood is planed, can also be used to create a realistic basket.

Fig. 11-8 Variation in strip width and color add interest to a simple design.

Fig. 11-9 The star and decorative bands are also forms of paper weaving.

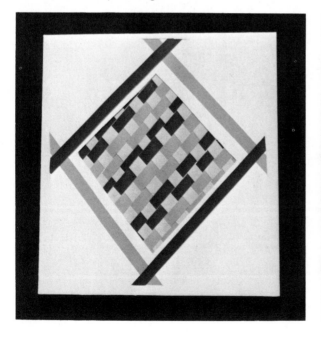

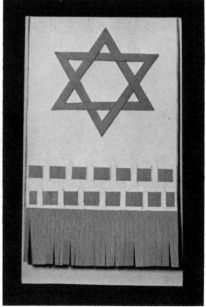

Pop-Ups 12

How to cut and fold paper to make three-dimensional pop-out cards

Open one of these cards and a friendly lion will hand you a flower. On another, a colorful cake pops out to say "Happy Birthday." And on another, a beach umbrella casts a shadow on a real sand beach. All of these cards are made with simple folds, cuts, and a few easy embellishments.

To help you create these three-dimensional cards-in-motion, we have included patterns and step-by-step instructions. You can copy them directly, or adapt the pop-up idea to an idea of your own.

Fig. 12-1 Birthday cake pop-up card.

Fig. 12-2 Birthday cake pop-up, inside.

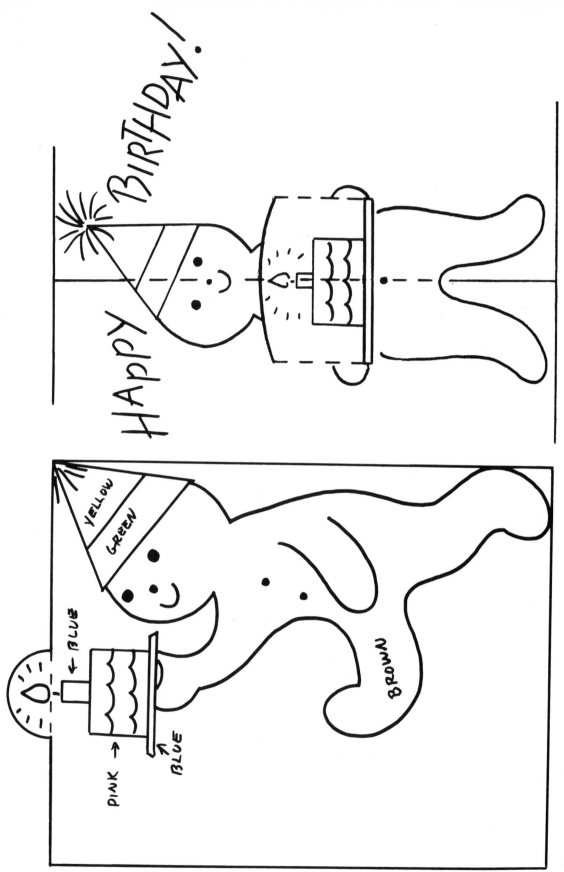

Fig. 12-4 Pattern for interior of the birthday cake card.

Fig. 12-3 Pattern for front of the birthday cake card.

Birthday Cake Card

Who said a card must be square or rectangular? This little card not only has a pop-up inside, it also highlights the happy gingerbread boy by placing him in dramatic silhouette (figs. 12-1 and 12-2).

This is a good basic design, and the birthday cake only illustrates one way the pop-up can be used. The cake could be a gaily wrapped package, or you can use a large inside pop-up to highlight the message. A little tinkering with paper and an X-acto knife and you should be able to come up with some interesting applications of this pop-up.

Materials

White paper for the card
Colored paper: brown, pink, yellow, green, and blue
Package of colored confetti
Tracing paper
Transfer paper
Marking pens: black (thin line), red, orange, and yellow
Scissors
Pencil
Rubber cement
X-acto knife

Directions

1. Prepare a French fold with a piece of 8½" x 11" white paper. After the fold lines have been created, open the paper and spread it out flat.

2. Trace the various colored parts shown in figs. 12-3 and 12-4 (use the same colors for the inside parts as for the outside ones), and transfer them to the appropriate colored paper. Cut out the parts and use rubber cement to position them as shown in fig. 12-5.

3. Now cut out the two pop-ups. Use a quarter as a guide to cut the semicircle on the inner page with an X-acto knife. When the card is folded, lift up the flap from the inside fold to highlight the candle on the front. Use an X-acto knife to prepare the cake pop-up. Cut the top and bottom of the cake (see fig. 12-6).

4. Re-fold the card along the lines made when the French fold was first prepared. Cut along the gingerbread boy's back, following the edge of the brown shape and the back of the hat. All pages of the card should be cut at the same time to create the

silhouette. To make sure that the cutting goes smoothly, hold the card tightly closed with your thumb and forefinger close to the point being cut. Move your fingers after each inch of cutting until the silhouette has been completed.

5. Lift up the semicircular flap that was cut out in step 3. Use the yellow marker to create the candle glow on this flap as well as on the cut-out candle inside.

6. Add red icing swirls to the cakes. Use the orange marker to

Fig. 12-5 Position for the parts of the card.

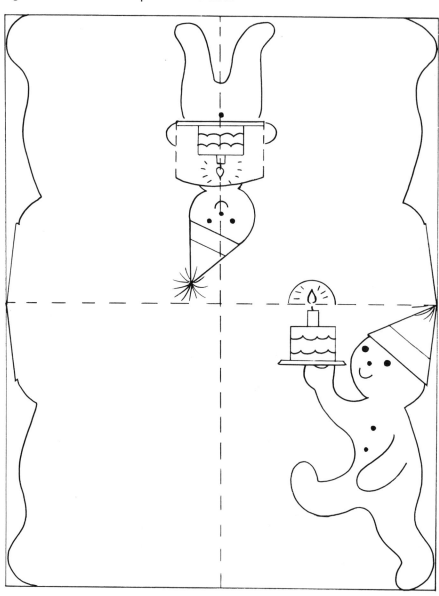

make the hat pom-pom as well as the candle flame. Use a black marker to draw the face, arms, buttons and candle wicks.

7. Fold out the cake on the inside of the card. Use the dotted lines as a guide. Hold a ruler along the dotted lines to make sure the folds are sharp. When folded, the cake will protrude out into the card. Open and close the card several times to make sure the pop-up works smoothly.

8. Use rubber cement to add the colored confetti, and add the "Happy Birthday" with a colored marker.

Friendly Lion Card

Made similarly to the birthday cake card, the pop-out bouquet in fig. 12-7 is a cheery gift from a friendly lion (or the animal of your choice). The lion is simply drawn on the front and interior of the card with marking pens, and cut-out construction paper flowers are glued in place. The pop-up is cut and folded out from the card paper *before* the flower is glued down on top of it.

Your card can say anything you want. "Come to a party" or

Fig. 12-6 Cut lines (heavy) and fold lines (dotted) for the pop-ups.

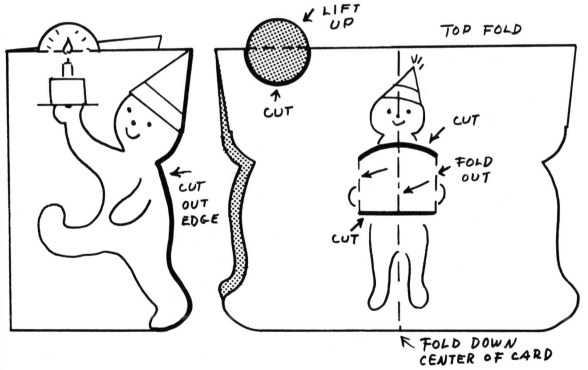

Fig. 12-7 Friendly lion card, inside.

Fig. 12-8 Flower petal pop-up card.

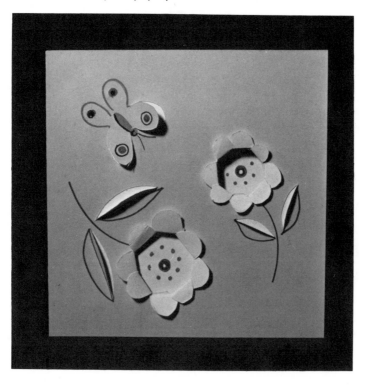

just "Thanks for being so nice" are possibilities. And you can use this pop-up principle in a number of other ways. For instance, instead of a flower, you could invite friends to a barbecue and make the pop-up look like a hamburger.

Flower Petal Pop-Up

Flowers open and butterfly wings spring to life when this card is pulled from its envelope (fig. 12-8; see also color photo 10). The movement is slight, but the feeling of depth present in this card is hard to find in commercial cards. This same principle can be applied to other ideas with interesting results. A bird's wing, flowers of other shapes, and any number of objects can be given dimension with this technique.

Our card measures 5″ x 5″ when folded and is made with a sheet of 10″ x 10″ paper. But you can adapt the design to an 8½″ x 11″ sheet, or to any size card you want.

Materials

White paper (one sheet 10″ x 10″ and another at least 5″ x 5″)
Bright yellow paper colored on one side only. (Or use any garden-fresh color you like.)
Pencil
Tracing paper
Transfer paper
Scissors
X-acto knife
Fine black marking pen
Colored marking pens
Rubber cement
Masking tape

Directions

1. Make a French fold of the 10″ x 10″ piece of white paper.
2. Make a tracing of the pattern shown in fig. 12-9.
3. Trace the patterns shown in fig. 12-10 on a separate piece of tracing paper. Lay this tracing over the tracing of fig. 12-9 to check the fit. Be sure that the petals of the two tracings overlap as seen in fig. 12-11.
4. Cut the yellow paper to 5″ x 5″, and transfer the tracing of fig. 12-9 to its colored side. Trace lightly.
5. Use an X-acto knife to cut all of the heavy lines and remove the shaded areas. Discard the scrap. Fold up the wings, leaves, and petals at the dotted lines. The yellow side of the

paper should face you and the white side of the pop-ups should be exposed. Fold the petals down flat.

6. Transfer the tracing of fig. 12-10 to a piece of plain white paper that has been cut to 5″ x 5″, or slightly smaller. Use an X-acto knife to cut out the shaded area.

7. Place the white-paper cut-out behind the yellow sheet so the petals of the white sheet can be seen through the yellow cut-out. Use small pieces of masking tape at opposite edges to hold the two pieces of paper together in the correct position. Now, pull the white petals up through the cut-out on the yellow sheet and press them down against the petals formed from the yellow paper. These petals should overlap each other, as can be seen in fig. 12-8.

8. Use rubber cement to join these two pieces of paper together. If any cement is visible after it dries under the butterfly

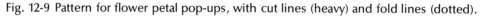

Fig. 12-9 Pattern for flower petal pop-ups, with cut lines (heavy) and fold lines (dotted).

Fig. 12-11 Put one tracing over the other to check the fit and make sure the petals overlap as shown.

Fig. 12-10 Pattern for second tracing, with cut lines (heavy) and fold lines (dotted).

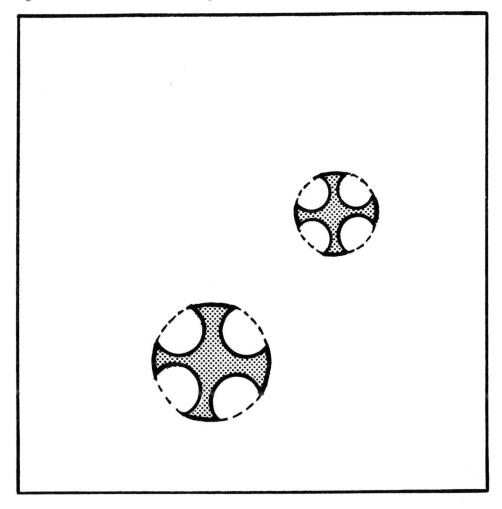

wings or the leaves of the flowers, just rub it off with the tip of your finger.

9. Use rubber cement to join this assembly to the front of the previously made French-fold card.

10. Use the black marking pen to outline the leaves and to draw the stems and butterfly wings. Create designs on the wings and the centers of the flowers with the colored pens.

11. Because this is an odd-size card, you may want to make your own envelope. Follow the envelope pattern in chapter 1, but change the dimensions to fit the card.

Sandy Beach Card

This amusing little card (fig. 12-12) was made with several pieces of summery colored paper—and a piece of ordinary sandpaper. To get the real effect of this card, see also color photo 10.

You might want to take the sandy beach idea and add your own details to the design—a paper boat pulled up on the beach, for instance, or, you might think of a way to make paper gulls strut on the beach and soar over the sea.

Fig. 12-12 Sandy beach card.

Materials

White Bristol paper
Bright yellow paper
Blue paper
Fine sandpaper
Rubber cement
Brown and red marking pens
Scissors
Pinking shears
Tracing paper
Transfer paper
Pencil
Masking tape
X-acto knife
Ruler

Directions

1. Trace the pattern of the basic card shape and umbrella from fig. 12-13 and transfer to a piece of white Bristol paper. Cut most of it with an X-acto knife and straight edge, but use pinking shears to make the sun's rays. Following the umbrella pattern, use an X-acto knife to cut along the heavy line at the bottom and slightly up the sides of the umbrella top.

2. Turn the card over. Trace the shape of the umbrella top, using the pattern in fig. 12-14, and transfer it to the front of the card. Lightly indicate with the pencil where the stripes will go, and then fill in the stripes with a red marking pen. Flop the tracing of fig. 12-13, and, using it as a guide, transfer the dotted lines lightly in pencil to the front of the umbrella.

3. Place a ruler along each dotted line on the umbrella. The ruler should be positioned along the outer edge so that most of the umbrella can be seen. Place your forefinger under the umbrella and press against the ruler. This will make the umbrella three dimensional. After the umbrella has been shaped, erase the lightly drawn pencil lines.

4. Trace the pattern of the sea from fig. 12-15 and transfer it to a piece of blue paper. Cut the outside shape with scissors, but use an X-acto knife to make the cut-out opening for the umbrella.

5. Position the blue sea background on the front bottom of the card, and test for fit. The sea should fit snugly up under the umbrella, and all the edges should be even. If the edges need trimming, use small pieces of masking tape at several points to

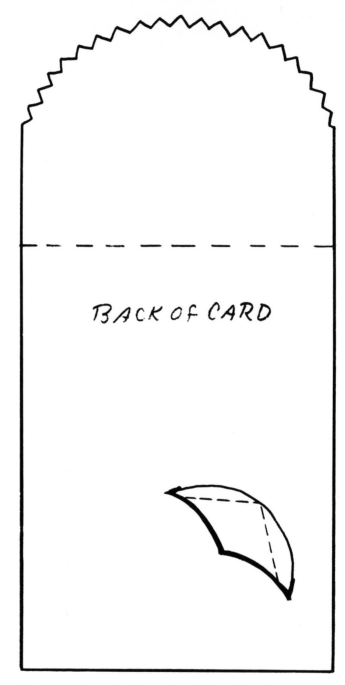

Fig. 12-13 Pattern for base of sandy beach card. This is the
back of the card.

Fig. 12-14 Pattern for umbrella and towel.

Fig. 12-15 Pattern for blue sea and opening for umbrella pop-up.

hold the sea in position while you use scissors to do the trimming. Once the fit is perfect, use rubber cement to attach the sea background to the bottom of the card.

6. Trace the sandpaper pattern from fig. 12-16. The sandpaper beach is just the bottom portion of this drawing; the rest shows the relation of the beach to the blue sea background. Flop the tracing before you transfer it (using transfer paper) to the *back* of the piece of sandpaper. Cut out the beach with scissors and make sure it fits perfectly at the bottom of the blue paper sea. Trim if necessary. Make sure the little nick in the beach fits snugly around the umbrella pop-up. Glue the beach in place.

7. Trace the towel pattern from fig. 12-14 and transfer to a piece of white paper. Cut out the towel and use a brown marking pen to make the fringe and a red pen for the two stripes. Use rubber cement to position the towel on the sandpaper beach.

8. Use the brown marking pen to draw the umbrella pole. (Draw this with a ruler.)

9. Trace the sun shape and face pattern from fig. 12-17 and transfer it to the yellow paper. Cut out the pattern and use the brown marking pen to draw the face.

Fig. 12-16 Pattern for sandpaper, and its position on the blue sea background.

SAND
(FINE SANDPAPER)

10. Turn over the part of the card with the sea and beach and lay it down opened and flat. Use rubber cement to attach the sun shape to the back of the card. Start applying the cement at the bottom of the back of the sun shape and work upward until the sun face is cemented in place on the Bristol.

11. Before the cement on the sun dries, fold the card forward to be sure the card will fold evenly later. After the cement dries,

Fig. 12-17 Pattern for sun shape and face.

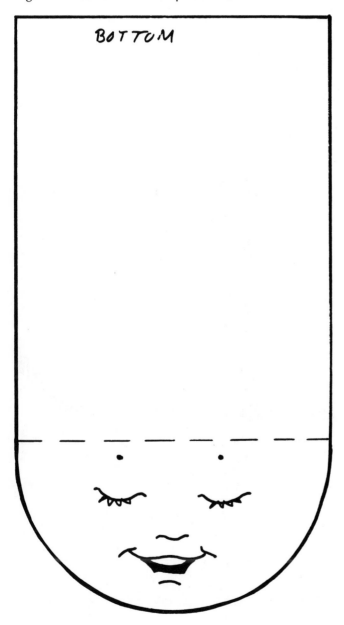

clean up any dried cement that may be exposed. Trim any uneven edges that may have occurred and erase any pencil lines that may still show. Write your message under the sun flap, above the blue sea.

Christmas Tree Ornament Card

Here's a Christmas card and a gift all in one (fig. 12-18 and color photo 12). Believe it or not, this elaborate card unrolls and can be sent flat through the mail. When it arrives, it is just rolled up and the string is tied to make a very pleasing three-dimensional tree decoration.

Materials

> White paper. Try to get a sheet that bends easily, but that is fairly sturdy. A piece of 100 lb. Bristol will do nicely.
> Colored paper

Fig. 12-18 Christmas tree ornament card.

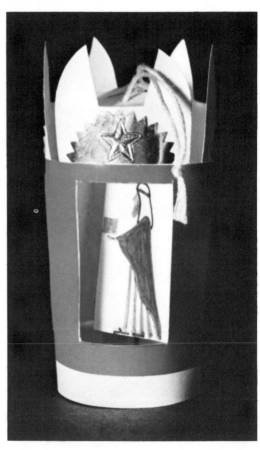

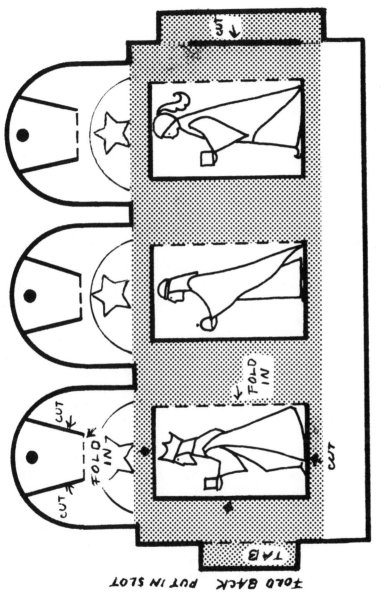

Fig. 12-19 Pattern for Christmas tree ornament.

Colored marking pens
Three 1¹/₂″ diameter gold notary seals
Colored stick-on stars (Dennison #225)
Colored yarn, string, or embroidery thread
Scissors
Pencil
Tracing paper
Transfer paper
X-acto knife
Straight edge
Rubber cement
Paper punch

Directions

1. Trace the pattern (fig. 12-19) and transfer it to the white Bristol paper.

2. Cut out the ornament outline.

3. Outline and color the wisemen, using the colored markers.

4. Trace and transfer the pattern of the color wrap-around (the shaded area in fig. 12-19) to a sheet of colored paper. Cut it out, and use rubber cement to attach it to the previously cut white Bristol sheet.

5. Cut the notary seals in half and glue them as indicated on the pattern. Glue the stars in place over the notary seals.

6. Cut the panels with the figures where indicated on the pattern with an X-acto knife and straight edge. Make three small holes on the top tabs for the hanging string and cut the slot for the tab on the right.

7. Run the string through the holes in the three tabs and roll up the card. The end tab should be fitted into the slot on the opposite side. When the string is tied, the card ornament will retain its shape (fig. 12-20). Push in slightly the cut-outs of the three wisemen.

8. The message can be written inside, or along the bottom if you don't mind it being seen when the ornament is hung on the tree. When you are ready to send the card, just untie the string (but leave it in the holes) and flatten it enough to fit in an envelope.

Fig. 12-20 Assembled ornament.

This window card (fig. 12-21 and color photo 10) uses a pop-up technique that is easy to do and is adaptable to cards for many occasions. Our card is a single fold, and a longer message can be written on the inside beneath the flowers and "Hello" greeting (fig. 12-22). Another way to use this idea is to glue your card shut, and have the entire message visible behind the pop-up. Or use several "windows," as done on the Advent calendars popular at Christmastime, and have different pictures or parts of your message behind each one.

Window-on-the-Garden Card

This card should be made with a piece of art paper colored on one side only, or with construction paper mounted on a white sheet. The white of the interior and on the back of the windows will then contrast nicely with the color of the outside of the card.

Materials

Colored art paper (or construction paper and white paper)
Colored construction paper
Tracing paper
Transfer paper
Pencil
Marking pens
Rubber cement
Scissors
X-acto knife
Straight edge

Directions

1. Cut the colored art paper to the size you want for a single-fold card, or else cut construction paper to the size of the card front and mount it on a single-folded piece of white paper.

Fig. 12-21 Window-on-the-garden card.

Fig. 12-22 Interior of the window-on-the-garden card.

2. Sketch your exterior and interior designs on tracing paper, and transfer them to the card. Your sketch should include the cut and fold lines for the windows. Figure 12-23 shows the arrangement of cut and fold lines used in our card.

3. Transfer other design elements (such as the fence, flowers, and butterfly in the card illustrated) to construction paper and cut them out.

4. Carefully cut the window on the front of the card with an X-acto knife and straight edge. When you cut the window, be sure the card is opened up, and you may want to pad your cutting surface with a piece of cardboard. After it's cut, open up the window and make a neat fold against the edge of the straight edge.

5. Attach your design elements inside and out with rubber cement. Position the inside elements carefully in relation to the window opening.

6. Add further embellishments and your message with the marking pens.

Fig. 12-23 Cut lines (heavy) and fold lines (dotted) for the shuttered window.

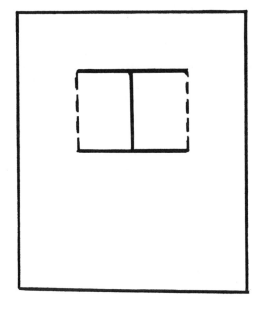

13 Chinese Tangrams

An oriental puzzle is the basis for endless geometric designs

Seven shapes, cut from one square, can provide you with an endless source of amusement as well as interesting patterns for cards. Called tangrams, the shapes originated in China and have been used and studied by both artists and mathematicians. The mathematicians are interested in ways of combining the elements to meet rigid specifications, but you, the artist, will probably find them more of a challenge to your sense of design.

The shapes of the tangram can be arranged to produce realistic designs, as we have done in the sailboat card (fig. 13-1). Or they can be assembled to produce unique nonobjective forms. Tangrams are the ideal doodler's device. Why not make up a set (cut apart a square according to the pattern in fig. 13-2) and have them lying around for those moments when you are at loose ends. Let your mind wander and arrange the pieces to suit your mood. When you are feeling expansive, the designs will be bold and forceful. In a quiet, contemplative period, you might find a tightly organized, gentle design. No matter what your mood, playing with tangrams is fun for everyone.

In addition to rearranging the basic shapes, you can play with color as well. Cut a set from several different sheets of colored paper. But, *never* use more elements in your arrangement than those used to make the original square.

94

Fig. 13-1 Sailboat card, based on a Chinese tangram.

Fig. 13-2 Tangram pattern.

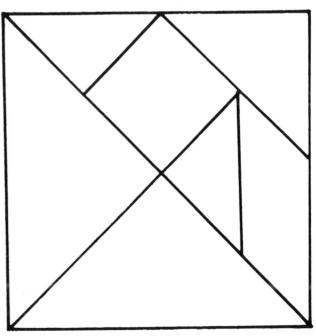

Sailboat Tangram

Your tangram can be arranged directly on the cardpaper, or on a separate sheet which will then be mounted on a card.

Materials

Several sheets of different colored paper
Tracing paper
Pencil
Straight edge
Carbon paper
X-acto knife
Paper for the card
Rubber cement

Directions

1. Draw the tangram figure on a piece of tracing paper (fig. 13-3).

2. Use the carbon paper to transfer the tangram to the colored paper (fig. 13-4).

3. Cut the tans apart using the X-acto knife and straight edge and arrange them on a sheet of paper to form the sailboat.

Fig. 13-3 Trace the tangram pattern.

Fig. 13-4 Transfer the tangram to a piece of colored paper.

When all the parts are arranged, make a dot under the corners of each tan to mark its position (fig. 13-5).

4. Use rubber cement to glue each tan in place (fig. 13-6).

5. Unless you have made your tangram design directly on the card, trim the sheet with the design on it and mount in on a single- or French-fold card.

More Ideas for Using Tangrams

In fig. 13-7, we have shown some other cards made of Chinese tangram designs. (These cards can also be seen in color photo 16.) On the shape of the poodle, we have drawn some curly lines and a smiling face with a black marking pen. Simple details like these can add a great deal of interest to your designs. The birthday greeting card is simply a nonobjective pattern of color and shape.

The tangram pieces can also be used to create landscapes, a butterfly, a flower blossom . . . the possibilities are endless, and you'll probably have more fun coming up with your own "originals." Remember, too, to think about the materials you use—very different effects can be created depending on the subtlety of the colors or type of papers you select.

Fig. 13-5 Arrange the shapes, and then put a small dot under each corner to mark their positions.

Fig. 13-6 Glue each piece in place with rubber cement.

You might want to make your design with the tans, glue them on a French fold and then cut away two or three sides of several of the tans to create lift-ups, under which you can write your message.

You can also use this Chinese puzzle in another interesting way: write your message on the tangram before you cut it apart, and mail the pieces to a friend. When they are assembled, your message can be read.

Fig. 13-7 More tangram cards.

Tissue Paper Pictures   14

How to rumple, crumple, and tear paper to make unusual cards

To make these cards, you tear, wrinkle, fold and pinch paper— and get a real chance to let your creative impulses out. Tissue paper can be bought in so many colors, that no card you make will ever be dull or uninteresting. You can tear paper and compose a realistic design, as was done with the landscape card in fig. 14-1. Or you can tear away at different colored papers and assemble the pieces in nonobjective patterns.

The card on the left in fig. 14-1 simulates a bouquet of roses, all from torn paper. To get the full effect of this technique, turn to photo 7 in the color section. Later in this chapter we will show you how to use the technique of quilling to make a different kind of tissue paper rose.

Fig. 14-1 Tissue paper pictures—always interesting and colorful.

Landscape Card

This card may seem to have an unusual color scheme—purple tree trunk, yellow sky, etc.—but it is a very effective one (see color photo 6) and actually quite representative of the glowing hues of a landscape at sunset. And, besides, clouds don't always have to be white, nor the sky blue. Your color scheme on any card can suit your fancy!

Materials

Blue and green tissue paper
Pink crepe paper
Purple and yellow construction paper
White paper for a French-fold card
White glue
Scissors
Rubber cement

Directions

1. Cut the yellow construction paper to the same size as the front of the card and use rubber cement to attach it to a French-fold card made of plain white paper.

2. The first elements to be pasted on the card are the clouds. Cut thin, random-shaped strips from the pink crepe paper and make an arrangement that pleases you. Mount the strips on the card with white glue.

3. The hint of blue for the rear ground shadows is next. Tear random pieces of blue tissue paper, rumple them, then spread them out and glue them in place with white glue. Do the same with the green tissue for more shadows behind the tree. This is one card which can benefit from a little glue showing. White glue dries clear, but it has a slight sheen. After you spread the glue over the shadow areas, on the sky, or on the tree foliage, the sheen will add yet another dimension to the landscape. And you will help prevent loose edges from lifting by spreading the glue thoroughly.

4. The tree trunk and mountains are cut with scissors from purple construction paper. You can tear them if you like, but the contrast of the sharp cut edge with the soft edge of the torn paper foliage and shadow makes an interesting effect. Use rubber cement to affix the mountain. The tree trunk is glued in place next, over the mountain.

5. Tear some green tissue paper to form the shape of the

foliage on the tree. When you have the shape you like, rumple the paper, spread it flat again, and glue it in place with white glue.

6. Tear another piece of green paper, roughly the same shape as that you made for the tree leaves, but about half the size. White glue this over the first piece of torn green paper. Tissue paper is translucent; when one piece is laid over another, the effect is a darker area. This will give your tree a feeling of depth.

7. Tear some more green tissue paper to form the shadow in the foreground in front of the tree. Overlap several strips to add texture and depth to this area. When you have the pieces you want, rumple the paper, spread it flat again, and then white glue the pieces in place.

This card, pictured on the left in fig. 14-1 and in color photo 7, is made from torn and folded papers. The materials are most of those used for the landscape card, plus a rose-colored marking pen or watercolor.

Folded Rose Bouquet

Materials

  Blue and green tissue paper
  Pink crepe paper
  Yellow construction paper
  White paper for a French-fold card
  White glue
  Scissors
  Rose-colored marking pen or watercolor
  Rubber cement

Directions

1. Cut the yellow construction paper to the same size as the front of the card and rubber cement it to a French-fold card made of the white paper.

2. Cut the crepe paper into 1" strips that are 6" long and follow the steps in fig. 14-2 to make the roses. Steps 3, 4, and 5 are also pictured in fig. 14-3. Once the roses have been formed, the "petals" (each fold) can be glued in place with small drops of white glue. The rose petals can be arranged so they are full and puffed up, or, if the card is to be mailed, they can be glued down tightly to fit in an envelope. Either way, you will not lose the character of the bloom.

3. Prepare the greenery background by tearing, rumpling, and

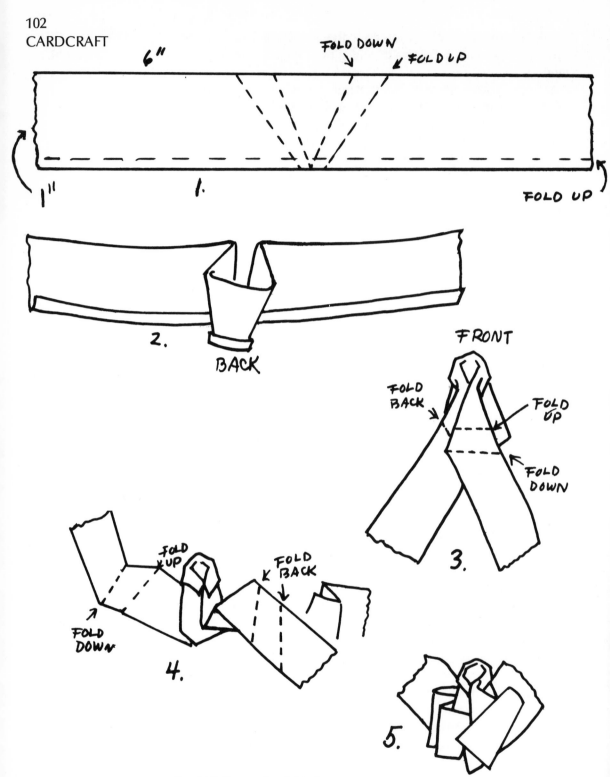

Fig. 14-2 Pattern for folded paper rose.

Fig. 14-3 Folding a paper rose. (The pins are used only to
help the folded paper pose for the picture.)

positioning pieces of green and blue tissue paper. Position the
blue paper first. The green should dominate; use only a random
hint of blue. Use white glue to attach the background paper.
Apply a little glue to the surface of the background paper, too.
When it dries, it will leave a light sheen.

4. Use white glue to attach the roses to the greenery background.

5. Using either the pen marker or watercolor, highlight the
center of each blossom with a small amount of rose color. Don't
overdo it; this is only to add detail and depth to the flower.

More Tips for Torn Tissue Cards

Remember when making cards with tissue paper that rumpling
the tissue paper will add texture and dimension, and that tearing
adds a softness to the edges of the design. You will be surprised
at how much interest these simple steps can add to the total effect of a card.

Torn tissue can also be used to make unusual backgrounds for
other cardmaking techniques. See color photo 7 for an example
of how a Styrofoam print was placed over a torn tissue background.

Miniature Rosebush
Small Blossoms

Quilling is an old technique of shaping paper that you can easily use to make paper roses. There are two ways to use this technique. The first way produces small, delicate roses and is illustrated by the card on the left in fig. 14-4. In this card, the roses are made by quilling, but the background—the pot, stalk, and leaves—is created with a marking pen and some green watercolor paint.

Materials

Pink tissue paper or quilling paper
Tracing paper
Pencil
Black marking pen (fine point)
Rose-colored marking pen or watercolor
Green watercolor
Small brush
White paper for design background and for French-fold card
Heavier colored paper for card front
Scissors
Pinking shears
Ribbon
White glue
Rubber cement
Hat pin (optional)

Directions

1. Using the pattern in fig. 14-5, trace the design onto white paper.

2. Outline the leaves and pot with the black marking pen.

3. Paint the leaves and stalk green with the watercolor. Don't fill each leaf with color; just a light stroke with white left around it will add interest and dimension.

4. Cut five strips of pink tissue paper, ³/₄" wide and 3" long. (If you prefer, you can use pre-cut quilling paper available at all craft stores.) Fold each strip twice, the long way; this will make the finished roses about ¹/₈" high.

5. Make the roses by holding one end tightly with the fingernails of your thumb and forefinger, and winding each strip tightly in a spiral (fig. 14-6). To make this part a little easier, you can wind each rose around the shank of a hatpin.

6. Use a dab of white glue at the end when you have finished winding the rose. You can hold each rose firmly while the glue is

Fig. 14-4 Cards with small and large quilled paper roses.

Fig. 14-5 Pattern for miniature rosebush card.

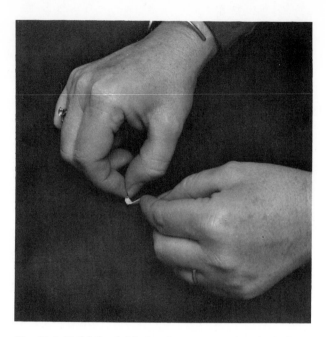

Fig. 14-6 Hold the folded strip at one end and wind the strip into a tight spiral.

drying by piercing the first few outer windings with a straight pin. Remove the pin carefully after the rose has dried.

7. Use white glue to attach the roses to the appropriate places on the design.

8. Place a dot of rose color (watercolor or marking pen) in the center of each rose.

9. Use pinking shears to trim the bottom of the colored paper.

10. Use rubber cement to mount the design to a piece of colored paper. Glue the ribbon over the top edge of the white paper on which the design has been made (see fig. 14-4).

11. Use rubber cement to mount the completed card-front to a French-folded white card.

Rambling Rose
Large Blossoms

The technique described for the miniature rosebush card produces small, delicate roses. You might think that to make larger roses, all you have to do is increase the dimensions. Not so! If you would like to make a card with larger, bolder blooms and with a three-dimensional stem, as on the rose vine card in fig. 14-4, follow the instructions below.

Materials

Pink crepe paper or quilling paper
Green tissue paper
Colored background paper
White paper for French-fold card
Pencil
White glue
Rubber cement
Toothpick
Scissors
Pinking shears
Rose-colored marking pen or watercolor

Directions

1. Trace the pattern in fig. 14-7 lightly onto colored paper.
2. Cut strips of pink crepe paper 8" long and ½" wide. Fold these strips twice, the long way.
3. Wind the roses tightly in a spiral. Begin by holding one end

Fig. 14-7 Pattern for rambling rose.

tightly with your fingernails and twisting. Keep the spiral flat between your thumb and forefinger as you wind (fig. 14-8).

4. Use a dab of white glue at the end of the strip to maintain the form of the bloom.

5. To make the stems, cut green tissue paper into strips of varying lengths, 1¼" wide. Twist the green strips very lightly (fig. 14-9).

6. Apply the stems to the background with white glue. Use a toothpick to spread the glue on the side of the stem that will contact the background paper.

7. Mount the roses as shown in the pattern. Apply white glue to the bottom of each rose with a toothpick.

8. Darken the center of each rose with watercolor or a rose-colored marking pen.

9. Trim the bottom of the colored paper with pinking shears. Mount the design on a French-fold white card. Leave a little white showing at the top and bottom as seen in fig. 14-4.

Fig. 14-8 Wind the folded strip into a flat spiral.

Fig. 14-9 To make the vine, lightly twist strips of green tissue paper.

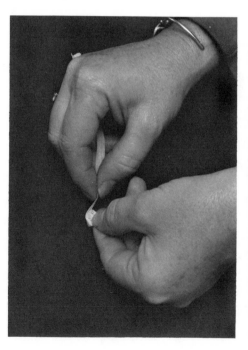

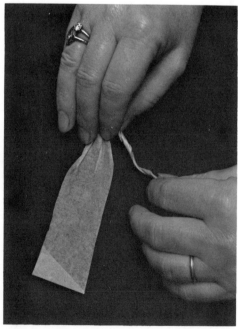

Embossing 15

How to give
your cards
a touch of elegance

A dramatic three-dimensional effect can be added to a card with nothing more than some foil or foil-faced paper, a paint brush handle, and some paper. The card we are about to describe (fig. 15-1) was made by using a piece of foil-faced paper salvaged from a commercial box or greeting card. These boxes are made by applying foil to one side, and they are most often available around holidays for special gift packaging.

However, if you are unable to find any foil-faced paper or greeting cards, you can emboss a card by using another technique, described later in this chapter, and some readily available kitchen foil. The reason for using the foil-faced paper is that the paper helps support and protect the embossed design.

Seals and emblems of great importance are often embossed, but the technique is ideal for showing off geometric designs like those found in Mexico and some of the African cultures. Of course, you can create your own patterns, whether realistic or nonobjective, and make them into an embossed design very easily.

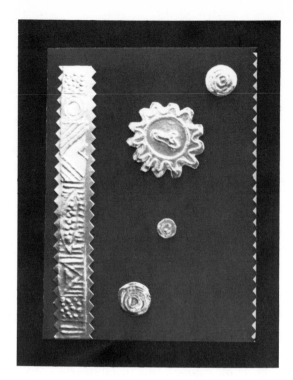

Fig. 15-1 Embossed card made with foil-faced paper.

Fig. 15-2 Pattern for embossed card.

The card in fig. 15-1 uses separately embossed elements which are glued to the face of the card. If you like, and if you can find enough foil-faced stock, you can emboss an entire card. The technique is limited only by the availability of the material and your own imagination.

Embossed Card
Using Foil-Faced Paper

Materials

Tracing paper
Carbon or transfer paper
Pencil
Foil-covered paper
Scissors
Pinking shears
Soft facial tissue
Small paint brush with a somewhat pointed but rounded-off end on the handle. You can substitute other embossing tools: an orangewood stick, the smooth cap of a ball-point pen, etc.
Colored paper for card front
White paper for a French-fold card
Rubber cement

Directions

1. Trace the pattern (fig. 15-2) and transfer it to the *back* of a piece of foil-faced paper. To transfer it, you can use carbon paper or a piece of homemade transfer paper, as described in chapter 1.

2. Cut out the individual shapes from the foil-faced paper. Use regular scissors to cut the round elements, and pinking shears for the rectangular shape.

3. Lay the shapes, *foil side down,* on a bed of three or four folded facial tissues. Using the embossing tool you have chosen, go over the lines of the traced pattern (fig. 15-3). Bear down enough so that the back of the paper is depressed and the embossed design appears on the foil side. If you are using exceptionally heavy stock, you may have to repeat the embossing several times to get a strong impression. However, be careful that you don't deform the paper beyond the stretch limits of the foil. Excessive pressure can rip the foil and ruin the project. It is best to try the embossing on a piece of scrap foil-paper first to determine how much pressure is needed and how much deformation the foil will tolerate.

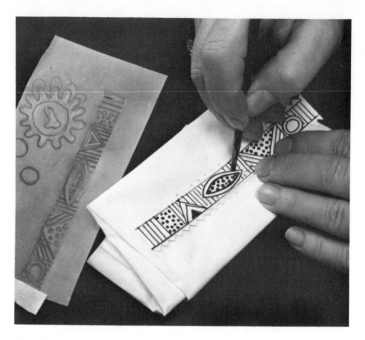

Fig. 15-3 Use the embossing tool to impress the pattern on the back of the foil-faced paper.

4. Cut a piece of colored paper to the same size as the front of your card. Using rubber cement, attach the embossed shapes to the colored sheet of paper.

5. Mount the color sheet with the embossed elements onto the front of a French-fold card.

6. Trim the long edge of the card with pinking shears just enough to expose the white paper. This flourish picks up the pattern of the embossed rectangle and completes the card.

Embossed Card
Using Kitchen Foil

If you have been unable to find any foil-faced stock, you can still make an embossed card with common kitchen foil. Kitchen foil is only available in a silver finish; if you would like to emboss a card with another color, colored foils are often available in craft supply stores.

Materials

Pencil
Tracing paper
Kitchen foil
Soft facial tissue

Embossing tool. A small paint brush handle, orangewood stick, or the smooth cap of a ballpoint pen are good for this.
White glue
Colored paper
White paper for French-fold card
Rubber cement
Sheet of cardboard, such as a pad backing
Scissors
Pinking shears

Directions

1. Copy the patterns on tracing paper. Transfer them to the plain aluminum kitchen foil by placing the foil on a piece of firm, flat cardboard, putting the tracing on the foil, and re-tracing the design with a pencil.

2. Cut out the individual shapes. Use regular scissors to cut the round elements, and pinking shears for the rectangular shape.

3. Lay the shapes on three or four folded facial tissues. Using the embossing tool you have chosen, go over the lines of the traced pattern. You will not have to bear down nearly as heavily as you did when you embossed the paper-backed foil. In fact, if you bear down too hard, you will rip the foil. It's best to make a test of the amount of pressure you can use before the foil rips.

Fig. 15-4 More embossed designs.

4. After you have completed the embossing, the foil will be fragile, and the slightest pressure could damage the pattern. Handle with care.

5. To protect the embossed pattern and make it useable, it will be necessary to reinforce it. Lay the embossed element face side down, and fill the exposed depressions with a heavy coating of white glue. The entire back of the foil should be covered with glue, but just pour it on—don't attempt to work it in with anything, or you will damage the embossing.

6. When the glue dries, you can use rubber cement to attach the embossed shapes to a colored sheet of paper. Then, follow steps 5 and 6 in the previous instructions for completing the card.

Embossed foil can be used in a number of ways. Some of them have been illustrated in fig. 15-4.

Postcards 16

*How to make your own postcards
using favorite pictures
or prints*

Who says that a greeting card must be sent in an envelope? With nothing more than a picture, some cardboard, dry mounting tissue, and an iron, you can make some very unusual postcards. And, of course, you save money on postage when you send postcards instead of a card in an envelope.

The illustrations can be anything you choose. A favorite photograph, an unusually interesting section of a piece of gift wrapping or wallpaper, a cartoon, or even a piece of sheet music that means something to you and the person who will get it. If you want to send the same thing to a number of friends (a cartoon for example), why not Xerox it, mount the copies, and send

Fig. 16-1 Just about any photograph or picture can be mounted to make
your own postcard.

them on their way? All of these ideas can be permanently mounted on cards and sent to friends.

Picture Postcard

Materials

Picture, photograph, or print

Dry-mount tissue (available at camera shops)

Oaktag, or index Bristol paper. This is a stiff sheet used to make index cards and file dividers. You can also use conventional file cards, or cut the cards you need from a file divider or folder.

Iron

White paper

Scissors

Directions

1. Select the photograph or picture you want to use. Be sure that it will meet the mailing size requirements. Some larger postcards are no longer mailable, so check with the Post Office for current regulations. If the picture is too large, it might be possible to trim it to a size that can be mailed. Most amateur photographs have more background than they need, and will actually benefit from a judicious amount of cropping.

Fig. 16-2 Stiff card paper, dry-mount tissue, and your picture stack up to make a mailable postcard.

Fig. 16-3 Lightly press the dry-mount tissue onto the back of the picture.

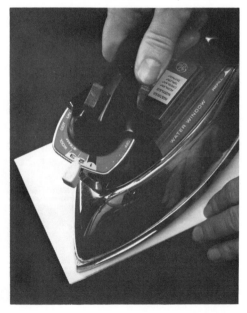

2. Cut a piece of index Bristol so that it is about ½" larger all around than the picture that is to be mounted on it. (The dry-mount tissue will be placed between the picture and the Bristol board; see fig. 16-2).

3. Trim a piece of dry-mount tissue to the same size as the photo. With the iron heated to the proper temperature (see Note below), lightly tack the dry-mount tissue to the back of the photograph (fig. 16-3). Be careful not to press down with the iron; let the heat only do the work.

Note: Temperatures required vary depending on the manufacturer and the material you are using the tissue with. There is a special tissue which fuses at a low temperature that is made for use with the new resin-coated photographic papers. If you use a conventional tissue with these papers and set the iron at the higher temperature, you will damage the photo emulsion. Proper temperatures and any special instructions are supplied with dry-mount tissue.

4. Position the picture with the attached dry-mount tissue in the middle of the Bristol board.

5. Place a piece of clean white paper over the surface of the photograph and iron the surface. *Do not* bear down heavily; let the heat and weight of the iron do the job. Be careful to keep the iron flat; if the tip digs in, you can damage the picture.

6. Lift the sheet of white paper and examine the seal. Flexing the board back and forth slightly will tell you if the seal has been fully made. If the seal is incomplete, you may hear a rippling as the paper is flexed. Just apply the paper and iron again.

7. After the seal has been made, trim away the excess Bristol board. Here's where a paper cutter can come in handy, but you can do the job with a pair of scissors or with an X-acto knife and a straight edge.

8. Rule the other side of the card in half, the short way. The left side can be used for the message and the right for an address.

More Postcard Tips

There are a number of other ways that you can make attractive postcards, in addition to the use of dry-mount tissue. Many of the techniques described in this book can be used effectively. For example, you can turn out a quantity of cards by using linoleum or Styrofoam block printing, or the silk screen process. For making one or a few cards, think about using batik, marking pen needlepoint, oil and water prints, or pasting down the Chinese tans in appropriate patterns.

17   Decoupage

How to make fancy-free cards with glue and just about anything else, plus how to make your own decals

A decoupage card can be as simple as the anniversary card shown in fig. 17-1 (see also color photo 17), which uses only a piece of ribbon and a sticker, or as elaborate as you want to make it. It is not necessary to clutter a card with everything you can find to make it attractive. There is beauty in simplicity, and it is a creative challenge to make a card with fewer, rather than more elements. For example, the birthday card shown in fig. 17-2 was made with one sticker, some paste-on letters, and two strokes of a white pencil on a piece of green paper.

Your card can be made on anything from a single sheet or French fold to an elaborately folded piece. Think of what you might be able to do with an accordion fold on which design elements or words are pasted sequentially. Unlike other cards,

Fig. 17-1 Simple decoupage anniversary card.

Fig. 17-2 A birthday greeting for a tennis fan—another simple use of decoupage.

Fig. 17-3 Rickrack chicks decorate this Easter greeting card.

Fig. 17-4 Pattern for Easter greeting card.

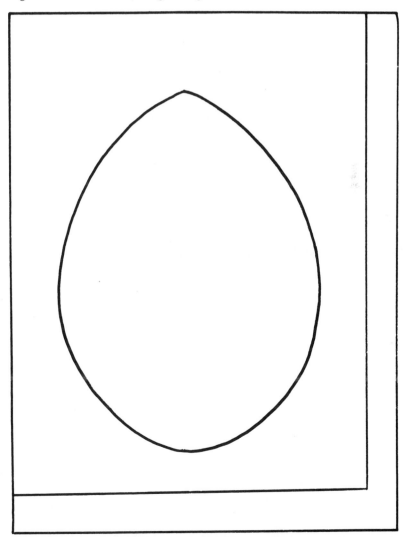

there are no specific materials needed. Let your imagination be your guide. But to help you, here are the items we used to make the cards illustrated in this chapter:

> Paper doilies or lace coasters
> Gold notary seals
> Rickrack
> Pictures cut from old cards and wrapping paper
> Lace hem binding
> Edging from a paper placemat
> Scraps of calico
> Self-adhesive protector pads (made by Avery)
> Dennison embossed seals
> Dennison pictorial seals
> E-Z self-adhering plastic letters

This cheerful Easter greeting (fig. 17-3 and color photo 14) has little rickrack chickens framed by a yellow egg cut-out.

Easter Greeting Card

Materials

Tracing paper
Pencil
Carbon or transfer paper
Yellow paper for egg cut-out
White paper for French-fold card
Scissors
X-acto knife
Rubber cement
Rickrack
White glue
Toothpick
White marking pen
Black marking pen

Directions

1. Using the pattern in fig. 17-4, trace the outline of the egg and the smaller of the two rectangles, and transfer the pattern to the yellow paper, using carbon or transfer paper as described in chapter 1.

2. Cut out the rectangle, and use an X-acto knife to cut out the egg shape.

3. With rubber cement, paste the egg cut-out to the front of a white, folded card. Note that the yellow piece with the egg cut-

out is smaller than the base card. Position the cut-out sheet flush with the top and left edges of the folded card.

4. Cut out the rickrack chickens. Use a toothpick to apply white glue to them and paste them in position.

5. Cut the rickrack edging to size and fix it to the card with white glue (fig. 17-6).

6. Use the white marking pen to put eyes on the chickens made with dark rickrack; use a black pen with light-colored rickrack. Add the feet to the white paper background with a black marker, and the card is finished.

More Ideas for Decoupage Cards

Let's take a look at some other possibilities for decorating cards with decoupage. The card in fig. 17-7 (see also photo 17 in the color insert) shows what can be made with a paper doily, some self-adhering letters, and a cut-out from an old card. The card in fig. 17-8 is somewhat more elaborate. The decorative element at the top was made from a gold paper coaster.

In fig. 17-9, the tree was made with Avery self-adhesive protective pads. The dots are Avery office codes. Gold rickrack, stars, colored paper tectangles, and a few more details complete the design.

Fig. 17-5 Trace the pattern and transfer it to the yellow paper.

Fig. 17-6 Spread white glue on the rickrack with a toothpick, and paste the pieces in position.

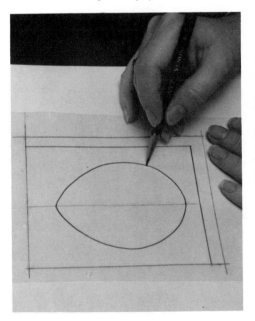

Fig. 17-7 A decoupage Valentine.

Fig. 17-8 An elaborate decoupage card made from well-chosen odds and ends.

In the cards in fig. 17-10 (see also color photo 15), swatches of cloth were used to make an interesting pattern. The cloth was attached with rubber cement. For interesting effects, trim the fabric with pinking shears, or pull out some threads to create fringe. The "stitches" on our card were made with black marking pen.

Because fabric can be found in such a variety of colors, textures, and finishes, the picture possibilities are virtually unlimited. Coarse burlap can serve as the side of a weathered barn, and a piece of flannel can be combed at the edges to produce the effect of a wind-blown pine tree. An old piece of corduroy might be turned into a board fence or a freshly plowed field. Try to match the characteristics of the cloth to the elements you have in mind for a picture, and some very interesting compositions are likely to result.

Making Your Own Decals

Anything goes with decoupage. In the cards we have illustrated, many of the elements were simple home findings—pictures, wrapping paper patterns, and so on. Decals are also fun to use, and you can add something special to any card by making your own. It's not as difficult as it may seem. Just follow these instructions.

Materials

Acrylic gloss medium
White typewriter paper
Colored marking pens
Rubber cement
Soft brush

Directions

1. Create your design on the white paper with the marking pens.

2. Use a soft brush to spread the acrylic gloss medium smoothly and evenly over the design.

3. Let the acrylic air dry, or you can hasten the process by putting the decal in an oven which has been set at the lowest temperature. Test the surface for dryness, and remove the decal from the oven when it is dry. You can spread a little gloss medium on a blank piece of paper to use when testing for dryness. This will keep fingerprints from the surface of the decal when testing. Let it cool to room temperature.

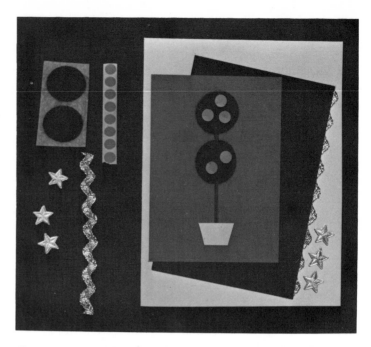

Fig. 17-9 Avery self-adhesive dots and protective pads, rickrack, stars, and construction paper add up to a unique decoupage design.

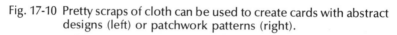

Fig. 17-10 Pretty scraps of cloth can be used to create cards with abstract designs (left) or patchwork patterns (right).

4. Place the decal, design side down, in a shallow dish of water. Let it soak for a minute or two.

5. When the paper has become thoroughly soaked, peel it away from the acrylic. The design will adhere to the acrylic, and you will have a semi-transparent decal that can be attached to a card with rubber cement.

18 Color Slide Cards

How to use slides and transparencies for cards that double as gifts

Natural light, some scraps of paper, and your favorite photographic color slide or transparency are all you need to make a special card for a special someone. Mounted in a simple frame and placed in a sunny window or beneath a table lamp, these cards add warmth and charm to any room (fig. 18-1).

Color slides, even if left in the dark, will fade over the years, and exposure to light hastens the process. But if you give a gift of food or drink, it can disappear much more quickly than the year it usually takes for a color transparency to loose its vibrance.

Rather than make the card from your original slide, you might

Fig. 18-1 A stand-up slide card—card and gift in one—will brighten a sunny corner.

have it copied. Duplicating a slide is a simple and relatively inexpensive process. Some slides are already large enough so that the image can be viewed without squinting. This is true of slides that are at least 2¹/₄″ square. However, most 35 mm slides will be difficult to see. For a truly exquisite card, you can have any size transparency enlarged by a photographic lab. Kodak Ektachrome slides can be blown-up to standard 4 x 5 or 8 x 10 sizes. If you want another size, it can be cut from a standard size.

You can frame the larger transparencies using the technique described below, or you might consider sandwiching an unframed transparency between two pieces of thin glass. When this is done, and the picture is then supported by a frame such as a Braquette, your sunny days will be even more cheery.

Fig. 18-2 Patterns for slide stands.

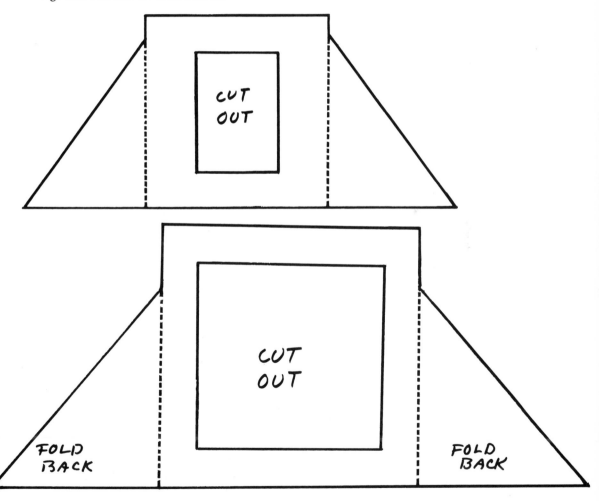

Stand-Up Slide Card

Materials

Slide (enlarged or actual size)
Ruler
Pencil
Heavy paper. Use colored or white paper depending on the color scheme of the picture and the room.
Tracing paper
Transfer paper
Rubber cement
Right triangle
X-acto knife
Toothpick

Directions

1. Measure the size of the cardboard frame on the slide. Measure both the outside and inside edges. Transfer the measurements to the heavy paper.

2. Use the X-acto knife to cut out the frame.

3. Trace the pattern for the slide stand (fig. 18-2). The patterns

Fig. 18-3 Ektachrome slide, heavy paper frame, and slide stand with written message will be glued together to make the slide card.

Fig. 18-4 To glue the parts together, carefully apply rubber cement with a toothpick.

we have provided are for 2¹/₄″ square, and 35 mm slides. Transfer the tracing to the heavy paper.

4. Use the X-acto knife to cut out the stand. Figure 18-3 shows the slide, paper frame, and stand.

5. Apply rubber cement with a toothpick when you assemble the slide, frame, and stand (fig. 18-4). The rubber cement bottle-brush can be a little clumsy, and you should try to avoid getting cement on the slide. The frame should be cemented to the *back* of the transparency; the stand is glued to the front.

6. Write your message on the flap of the stand and fold in the wings.

More Tips for Slide Cards

Because a slide card is rather personal, you will probably deliver it yourself. But if you plan to mail it, it would be wise to put a sheet of heavy cardboard on both sides before inserting it in the envelope. The backing from an ordinary legal pad will do very well. But don't leave anything to chance. Mark the envelope clearly: *Photograph—do not bend.*

If you want to provide a far-away friend with more than words when you write, why not consider making these slide cards regularly and at appropriate times. Birthdays, holidays, the changes of the seasons, and other events are all appropriate times to make and send these slide cards. And the friends to whom you send them will have an on-going reminder of you in pictures.

You can use a number of other materials besides plain paper to make the frames. Scraps of wall paper, balsa wood, and paper printed with the oil and water technique described in chapter 8 will work nicely. You might try gluing a piece of fabric to the paper frame for an interesting effect. When this is done, the cloth should be turned over the edges of the frame to ensure a smooth appearance.

The teacher who is stuck for a holiday idea can take advantage of this card. And if teachers in the succeeding grades follow suit, parents will have a yearly record of their children as they grow up.

19 String and Yarn Designs

How to string up a unique design with pieces of thread, cord, or yarn

If you're a string saver, these are the cards for you. Everything from straight-line geometrics to a gentle blending of soft line, color, and texture can be accomplished with very little effort. The cards we have illustrated in this chapter represent both ends of the design spectrum.

With a little imagination, you can use string and yarn to make realistic pictures—faces, scenes, and flowers are popular motifs. And by arranging different materials to suit your eye, you can create some fascinating nonobjective designs, too. Figure 19-1 il-

Fig. 19-1 String and yarn arranged in a flowing, nonobjective design.

Fig. 19-2 Shamrock card, "drawn" with white yarn on a green background.

lustrates a nonobjective design that made use of different sizes of yarn and string, and blended color with a gently sweeping line to create an interesting pattern. This card can also be seen in color photo 19.

If you enjoy the interaction of straight line, color, and sharp geometric forms, consider trying your hand with a thread card. In this form a basic pattern is created by making a cut-out in paper and then developing geometric designs in the openings with threads of different colors. This kind of card is described later in this chapter.

You can also develop motifs which represent a special occasion. The simple shamrock (fig. 19-2), made of white yarn on a

Fig. 19-3 Pattern for shamrock card.

green background, says happy Saint Patrick's Day to any Irish friend.

Shamrock Card

Materials

Yarn
Pencil
Tracing paper
Carbon or transfer paper
Colored paper
Spray starch
White paper for a French-fold card
Self-adhering office dot labels
White glue
Rubber cement
Toothpick
Scissors
Iron

Directions

1. Trace our pattern (fig. 19-3), or create your own design on tracing paper which has been ruled to the size of the finished card (fig. 19-4).

2. Transfer the design to the colored paper on which the yarn design is to be made, using carbon or transfer paper as described in chapter 1.

Fig. 19-4 Draw your design on tracing paper that is ruled to the size of your card.

Fig. 19-5 Press the yarn down on the thin line of glue.

3. Cut a piece of yarn long enough for the design. Spray some starch on the yarn and iron it lightly. This will straighten it and give it body to make it more manageable when you are forming the design.

4. Cut the scalloped edge on the colored paper and use rubber cement to glue it to the front of a white, French-fold card.

5. Trace over the outline on the card with a toothpick dipped in white glue. Keep the glue-line thin.

6. Form the yarn over the glue line, pressing lightly to ensure that the entire length is glued down (fig. 19-5).

7. Put the self-adhering office label dots in place along the scalloped border, as seen in fig. 19-2.

Geometric String Card

Materials

Thread in several colors
Tracing paper
Carbon or transfer paper
Pencil
Colored poster board
Colored paper
Masking tape
White paper for a French-fold card
Scissors
X-acto knife
Straight edge

Directions

1. To make a string design with geometric cut-outs like that shown in fig. 19-6 (see also color photo 19), first draw your design on tracing paper that has been ruled to the size of your card. Although you can make your cut-outs in a piece of paper that is exactly the same size as the front of your card, it is often more interesting to cut the colored papers to a different size or shape than the front of the card and use the blending of shapes and sizes as part of the design. Note in fig. 19-6 that three layers of paper show on top—the white of the card and two colored sheets. Note, too, that the shallow wedge cut out of the bottom edge of the top sheet complements the triangle motif and adds interest to the borders.

Your tracing paper design will be simply a single sheet of paper showing the outlines of the borders and cut-outs that you want on your card.

2. Transfer your tracing paper design to the colored poster board with carbon paper or transfer paper, as described in chapter 1.

3. Use the X-acto knife and straight edge to cut the poster board to size and to cut out the openings in it.

4. Stretch different colored threads across the backs of the openings to create your own design. Hold the thread in place with masking tape (fig. 19-7).

5. Using rubber cement, glue the assembled design onto a piece of colored paper. Pick a color that complements the colors of the poster board and threads. Now mount this on a French-fold card.

Another Idea for String Designs

If you found the yarn cards fun to make, you might want to try working in heroic proportions. You can color pieces of rope with clothing dye and create unique wall hangings by assembling the rope on cardboard, Masonite, or even on a piece of fabric. Think of using a coarse burlap as the background, and both fine- and rough-textured rope to create your designs. If your project is large, you should use fine wire to hold the rope in place, in addition to the glue. Run the wire through the background material and just catch the back of the rope where it is glued. You can also sew the rope in place at strategic points. Such a wallpiece may be the largest card one of your friends will ever get, but it will surely be the most memorable.

Fig. 19-6 A geometric design with string and cut-outs.

Fig. 19-7 Stretch threads across the backs of the cut-outs and hold them in place with masking tape.

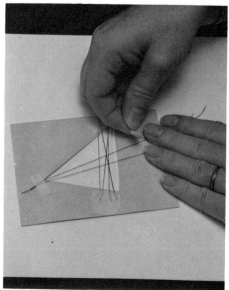

Stitched and Sewn Cards   20

How to sew a card —with simple stitches anyone can do

These are the cards that so many people save and frame. Whether it is made by hand or on a sewing machine, the sewn card is one of the most popular greetings you can create. Oddly enough, it's not important to be a good sewer to make these cards. The skills required to do good needlework are not necessarily those needed to create a card. Even if you've done very little sewing, with a little practice you can make some attractive cards. However, you should practice on scraps of cloth before you go on to make a finished card. Get the technique down, and your finished cards will make a hit with all who get them.

There are a number of ways to make sewn cards, but we have limited this section to a discussion of machine-sewn and hand-made cards using the running and outline backstitch. Let's begin with a simple card you can make on a sewing machine.

Fig. 20-1 Machine embroidery creates a plump little fir tree.

Fig. 20-2 Pattern for tree and tub.

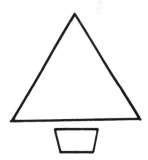

135

Machine-Embroidered Fir Tree Card

This card has a very simple design (fig. 20-1; see also color photo 20), but any of the patterns in chapter 25 can be used and filled in the same way. Only two colors were used, but as your skills develop, you can experiment with many different colored threads to create unusual effects.

Materials

Sewing machine with a zigzag attachment and an embroidery setting
Tracing paper
Pencil
Black marking pen
A piece of organdy
Embroidery hoop
Mercerized cotton thread
Colored and white paper
Rubber cement
Scissors

Fig. 20-3 Trace the design onto a piece of organdy that is stretched in an embroidery hoop.

Fig. 20-4 Remove the pressure foot, set the machine for embroidery, and place the organdy under the needle.

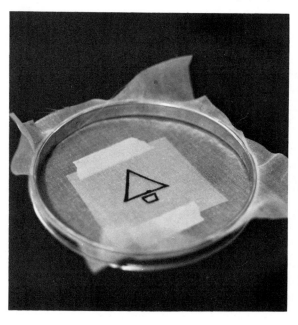

Directions

1. Trace the pattern of the tree (fig. 20-2), or draw your own design, on a piece of tracing paper.

2. Place some organdy into an embroidery hoop and turn it upside down. The hoop will be in the opposite position from that used for hand embroidery.

3. Trace the tree and tub outline onto the organdy, using the black marking pen. The black line will make a good guide for your sewing and will emphasize the design (fig. 20-3).

4. Remove the pressure foot from the sewing machine, set it for embroidery, and position the organdy pattern under the sewing machine needle (fig. 20-4). Set the stitch for a $1/8''$ zigzag.

5. Lower the pressure bar and slowly stitch within the inked tree pattern. Stitch all around the outside and then fill in the inside of the tree. You may have to go over to fill in some spots, but because this is a random texture it will not be noticed.

6. When the tree has been stitched, use the same technique with another color thread to create the tub. When the pattern has been sewn, remove it from the embroidery hoop.

7. Cut a piece of colored paper to the same size as the front of your card. Then cut a small square or rectangle from it to frame the embroidered design. Cut the organdy to fit behind the cut-out and use rubber cement to attach the sewn cloth to the back of the cut-out. Mount the framed design on a French-fold card.

Hand-Sewn Cards

Simple hand stitches can be used to create many attractive card designs. For the two cards pictured in figs. 20-5 and 20-6 (they also appear in color photo 20), we used only the running stitch and the backstitch. But, obviously, there are a number of other stitches that can be used to create interesting sewn cards. A small sampler can be made with a cross stitch, for example. These other stitches can be found in most basic sewing books.

Materials

Mercerized cotton thread
Regular sewing needle
Heavy cotton, linen, or felt
Tracing paper
Carbon or transfer paper
Soft pencil
Scissors

Stiff paper
Paper for the base card
Masking tape
Artgum eraser
White glue
Rubber cement

Directions

1. Trace the pattern (fig. 20-7 or fig. 20-8), or create your own, and transfer it to the cloth. (The desert scene was sewn on linen; the clover on a piece of felt.) Use a soft pencil and carbon or transfer paper to *lightly* transfer the design, as described in chapter 1. The design should be just barely visible on the cloth.

2. The outlines in both cards were done with the backstitch; the texture and the shadow at the base of the cactus and the clover leaf interior were produced with the running stitch (see fig. 20-9). If the material you are using begins to fray as you sew, use masking tape on the edges to hold the threads in place.

3. After your stitched design is completed, trim the cloth and mount it on your card. Because there are no fraying problems

Fig. 20-5 Hand-stitched desert landscape on a linen background.

Fig. 20-6 Clover leaf and blossoms, hand-stitched on a felt background.

Fig. 20-7 Pattern for desert landscape.

Fig. 20-8 Pattern for clover leaf and blossoms.

Fig. 20-9 The back-
stitch (top)
and running
stitch (bot-
tom).

with felt, it can be trimmed with pinking shears and mounted directly to the face of a card with rubber cement. The card sewn
on linen was mounted on a piece of stiff paper. The cloth was
turned over the edges of the stiff paper, glued in place with
white glue, and then the whole thing was glued to the face of a
card with rubber cement.

If you would like to have a fringe effect with a cloth such as
linen, tug lightly at the edges to create it. Once you have the
desired length of fringe, use some white glue on the back of the
cloth along the edges to prevent further fraying.

4. If any of the pencil outline is visible after the sewing has
been completed, remove it with a light rubbing of artgum.

Cards from Mother Nature 21

*How to use dried flowers
and other
natural materials*

A bouquet of dried flowers will keep the glow of summer alive through the long winters. Similarly, you can preserve the beauty of any season on a card. It is even possible to capture the natural mood of the seashore with as little as a pinch of sand, as you will see later in this chapter.

We have seen many natural cards that have been framed as pictures. So try to plan your card so that only the design appears on the front; keep the message on the back or inside.

There are several ways to make cards with flowers and leaves, but they all begin with dried flowers. So before we get into the details of natural cardmaking, here's one way to prepare the flowers and leaves.

How to Dry Flowers and Leaves

Flowers for display in a bouquet are dried so that they retain their shape, but when you use them on a card, you will want them to be pressed flat. This method is quick and effective.

1. Place ten to fifteen sheets of newspaper on a flat area and cover them with two layers of opened facial tissue. Make sure that the newspaper and the tissue are flat and that no folds will interfere when the flowers are positioned.

2. Place the flowers on the tissue, and space them at least an inch or two from each other.

3. Cover the flowers with another layer of tissue.

4. Cover the second layer of tissue with another ten sheets of flat newspaper.

5. Place a heavy book on top, and check the drying progress every few days. Some flowers will dry faster than others. Remove the dried flowers, and leave those that haven't dried for another few days.

6. After the flowers have dried, you may want to give them a light spray of clear plastic. These spray finishes are available at

Fig. 21-1 An arrangement of dried flowers and leaves
makes a graceful greeting card.

Fig. 21-2 More arrangements of dried blossoms, leaves, and colored papers.

craft and hobby stores. It is especially important to spray the more delicate flowers to keep out moisture. The flowers are now ready to be used in your cardmaking.

Although many flowers and leaves can be dried and used, you will find that some hold color better than others and that some will be more appropriate for the theme of the card. A little testing of the leaves and flowers in your area will give you an idea of the materials that will be best for you. Not only are the colorful blooms of summer ideal, but autumn foliage can also be captured and used in your cards.

Here are some of the flowers that are more easily dried and that offer a variety of color and shapes: pansies, marigolds, forget-me-not, honeysuckle, goldenrod, scotch broom, violets, white violets, daisies, larkspur, phlox, jewelweed, buttercups, black-eyed susans, and weeds. These leaves dry well: pistache, poplar, ginko, dogwood, mulberry, white birch, beech, sweet gum, willow, and wild ferns.

Using the technique described below, you can make cards with your own arrangements of flowers and leaves, like those shown in figs. 21-1 and 21-2. (See also photo 21 in the color insert.)

Flower Garden Greeting Cards

Materials

Dried flowers and leaves
Tweezers
Scissors
Hard pencil
Toothpicks
White glue
Paper for the card

Directions

1. Select the best-looking dried flowers and leaves. If you plan to use a colored paper, choose one whose color enhances the flowers.

2. Decide on the dimensions you want, and cut and fold the paper for the card. If you plan to write on the inside, use a French fold, because the thickness of the flowers can interfere with writing.

3. Arrange the flowers and leaves on the front of the card. Try overlapping the flowers and leaves to add a feeling of depth.

4. Make light pencil marks *under* the leaves and flowers at key points (fig. 21-3). If you are going to overlap any of the elements, you should make a separate sketch for the order in which the pieces will be glued in place.

5. Using the toothpick, apply a light dab of white glue to the back of each flower or leaf, and position it with the tweezers (fig. 21-4).

6. After each flower and leaf has been glued down, look for loose parts that may fall off or that can be easily knocked off when the card is slid in and out of the envelope. Glue these parts down, and the card is complete.

7. This card is rather fragile. If it is to be sent in the mail, protect it by inserting in the envelope a piece of heavy cardboard the same size as the card, and cover the face of the card with light tracing or typing paper.

Sealed Flower Cards

These cards are made by applying a sheet of self-sealing plastic over a flower arrangement (fig. 21-5). These plastic sheets are available in most office supply stores and craft stores. Only dried flowers should be used, but you can use fresh leaves or hemlock for this card.

Fig. 21-3 Make light dots with a pencil to mark the position of each piece.

Fig. 21-4 Put a dab of glue on the back of each piece and position it with tweezers.

Materials

Dried flowers and fresh or dried leaves
Hard pencil
Scissors
Toothpick
White glue
Tweezers
Rubber cement
Self-sealing plastic sheets
White paper for the flower background
Colored paper for the card

Directions

1. Fold the colored paper to the finished size of the card.

2. Position the dried flowers and leaves on the white paper. To hold it in place while the plastic is being applied, use a toothpick to place a tiny dab of white glue under each part, and position them with the tweezers.

3. Cut the plastic to size, and carefully cover the flower and the sheet with it. Once this plastic touches the paper, it cannot be lifted up again, so make sure that you have it in the right

Fig. 21-5 This flower is protected with a sheet of self-adhering plastic.

Fig. 21-6 Carefully lay the plastic down, beginning at one end of the paper.

position. The plastic is easiest to apply if you start with one end and gradually lower the sheet until the paper is covered (fig. 21-6). Press down on the plastic around the edges of the flower.

4. Trim the paper on which the flower is mounted, and use rubber cement to glue it down on the colored stock you have selected. Adding a strip of white paper is a final embellishment.

Seascape

This card (fig. 21-7; see also color photo 21) uses nothing but paper and sand. For other design ideas, you might consider using bird seed or any other granular material.

Materials

Colored paper
Stencil paper
White paper for the base card
Pencil
Masking tape
Sand
White glue
Rubber cement
Scissors
X-acto knife

Fig. 21-8 Position the stencil, spread the glue, and sprinkle on the sand.

Fig. 21-7 Seascape with a real sand beach.

Directions

1. Begin by designing your card with paper and pencil.

2. Trace the outlines of the areas that are to be covered with sand onto stencil paper, and use the X-acto knife to cut out these areas.

3. Cut the colored background to the size you want for the scene's background. Place the stencil in position over the colored paper, secure it with masking tape, and apply a liberal coating of white glue.

4. Sprinkle the sand over the glue (fig. 21-8). Rub the sand lightly to make sure that you have an even coating and that all the grains are being held by the glue. Lift the stencil and let the glue dry.

5. Cut the parts for the rest of your design from colored or white paper. Apply the cut-outs to the card with rubber cement.

6. With rubber cement, glue the scene onto the folded card.

22 Lettering

Making the message —with hand lettering and press-on type

Lettering is where many people have the most trouble with handcrafted cards. Don't despair—some of the most talented artists simply cannot do lettering. In fact, the major greeting card publishers employ people who do nothing but lettering, leaving other artists to do the design and finished art. However, if you keep your lettering style simple and don't try to simulate finished calligraphy or typography, you will have very little trouble.

We have included several simple alphabets that you can trace or copy. The styles of the letters are usable with a wide range of artwork, and the message to accompany most of the cards in this book can be lettered with them.

The illustrated alphabets are not meant to simulate precise typography; they are hand-lettered. After all, your cards will be handmade and the message style should be compatible with the artwork.

Selecting a style of lettering for a particular greeting card is a matter of compatibility. For example, if you are planning to make a card with a bold, angular motif, you should think of using a similarly styled lettering, one which is angular, has no roundness whatsoever, and in which all the strokes are of the same weight. Such lettering is formal in appearance and is seldom used with a card that is sentimental in visual tone and content. On the other hand, a flowery or sentimental card is enhanced with lettering done in a cursive style.

Seldom does the lettering overpower the illustration, except in the novelty, studio-type cards. To get a feel for how lettering is used on different cards, you might want to visit a stationery store and look at a number of different cards.

If your card is to include a lettered message, do a sketch of the card design with the rough lettering on it. As long as you know the position the lettering and art elements will occupy, the

ABCDE
FGHIJK
LMNOPQ
RSTUV
WXYZ

ABCDEFGHI
JKLMNOPQ
RSTUVWXYZ
abcdefghijklm
nopqrstuvwxyz

abcdefghijklmnopqrstuvwxyz

abcdefghijklmnopqrstuvwxyz

abcdefghijklmnopqrstuvwxyz

ABCDEFGHIJKLMNOPQR
STUVWXYZ

lettering can be done at any time during the cardmaking process. If you are lettering by hand, you can space the letters to suit your design. But if you are using paste-on letters (described later in this chapter), you should make sure the message fits by actually measuring the letters and spaces that will be used. Make a tracing of the letters as they will be arranged and transfer the sketch lightly to the card. This will insure that all elements fit before you begin the artwork.

Hand-Lettered Card

The simplest card is nothing more than a lightly embellished message (fig. 22-1). This is the kind of a card we have chosen to describe a simple lettering technique.

Materials

Paper for the card
Tracing paper
Transfer paper
Right triangle
Soft pencil
Masking tape
Kneaded eraser
Colored marking pens

Fig. 22-1 Simple can be best.

Directions

1. Draw the dimensions of the card on tracing paper. Use the triangle to square up the corners.

2. On a separate piece of tracing paper, draw lettering guidelines to position the tops and bottoms of your letters. Use the triangle to make sure the lines are parallel.

3. Lay this piece of paper over the first and sketch in lightly where you want the lettering to be. You can trace from one of the alphabets we have included or draw your own letters freehand. Use your eye to test for the best placement—it may be necessary to cut and move the various elements until you have what you want. When you have a pleasant arrangement, tape the pieces in place (fig. 22-2). Use the triangle to check the alignment of the lettering again.

4. Pencil in a design, such as the simple flowers we have used, on the tracing.

5. Transfer the design to the card paper, using a soft pencil transfer paper as described in chapter 1 (fig. 22-3). Or else you can hold the card and tracing paper to a well-lighted window, and trace the design directly with marking pens. If you choose to use the transfer paper, lighten the transferred lines with a kneaded eraser so they are just barely visible. Then go over the design with colored marking pens. Marking pen ink is translucent, and unless you are careful, the pencil lines may show.

Transfer Letters

There are others ways to get your message across, without lettering by hand. One way to do it is with pre-printed transfer letters. These letters are printed in a waxy substance on a plastic backing and are available in many styles and sizes at most art supply stores. You simply position the letter, rub the back of the sheet, and the letter comes off the backing and onto your card. These letters are used by commercial artists, and the effect can be very pleasant, as well as professional. However, the letters are rather fragile and can crack even after you've put them on the card, but you can protect them by spraying on a light coating of fixative, such as Krylon. Several light coats are better than one heavy one. Let each coating dry before you apply the next.

Materials

A sheet of transfer letters

Burnisher. The back of a smooth spoon handle is remarkably effective; burnishers can also be bought in art supply stores.

Tracing paper

Transfer paper

Fig. 22-2 When you have sketched the position of your letters, tape the sketch down onto the tracing paper outline of the card.

Pencil
Straight edge
Paper for card
Spray coating, such as Krylon

Directions

1. First make a tracing-paper layout of the position of the lettering to make sure it will fit in the space you have. To do this, draw an outline of the card on tracing paper and then draw guidelines to position the tops and bottoms of the letters you plan to use. Be sure to plan for the spacing between lines of letters if your message will take up more than one line.

2. Place the ruled tracing paper over the sheet of transfer letters and trace each letter in the message. *Caution:* Use a very soft pencil to do this, and do not bear down, or you might loosen or damage the letters. Make any adjustments you feel are needed to make the lettering look good. Check the evenness of spacing between letters and between words.

3. Transfer the tracing-paper guidelines at the bottom of each row of sketched letters to the proper position on the card.

4. If you are making a French-fold card, it is best to apply the press-on letters with the card in the opened position. Fold the

Fig. 22-3 Transfer the design to the card paper using homemade transfer paper.

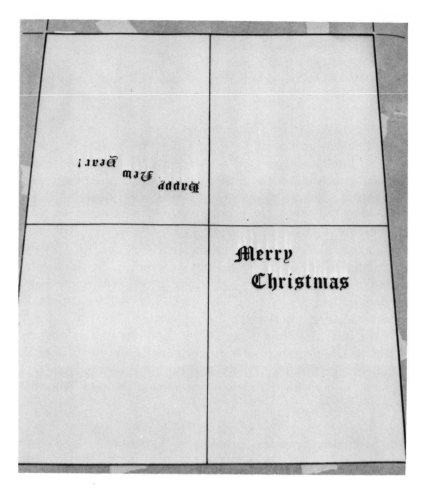

Fig. 22-4 Transfer letters are used for the message on the front and inside of this French-fold card.

card first, but then unfold it for the lettering process. If the type is rubbed into position inside a *folded* card, type which has already been placed on the front could be damaged by the pressure and rubbing. Be sure that the lettering appears in the right panels, and that the inside lettering is applied correctly. For the inside letters to appear right side up when the card is folded, they must be applied upside down when the card is unfolded (see fig. 22-4).

5. Position each letter on the card, following the guideline and the tracing paper layout. The letter is transferred from the sheet to the card by rubbing the back of the sheet with the burnisher while holding the sheet in position (fig. 22-5). Before you lift the sheet completely after rubbing down a letter, raise it a

little bit at a time to make sure all the letter has been transferred. If any of the letter is still adhering to the sheet, lay it down gently and rub the area that still adheres to the sheet.

6. After the lettering is complete, carefully erase the guidelines and apply several light coats of Krylon to the type. Cover any illustrations so the Krylon doesn't coat them.

There is yet another way you can have the effect of professional lettering. Super Stick letters, made by E-Z Letter, and similar letters made by other manufacturers, come with self-adhesive backings, and all you have to do is peel them from the backing and press them in position. These letters are available in a number of sizes and colors and are sold in art and stationery supply stores. The tennis motif birthday card shown in chapter 17 was made with these letters.

Stick-On Letters

Fig. 22-5 Match up the guidelines and rub the letter in place.

Materials

A sheet of stick-on letters
Pencil
Straight edge
Tweezers
Card ready for lettering

Directions

1. Draw a pencil guideline on the card where you want to position the type.

2. To judge where to place the letters, estimate the length of the type line by counting the number of letters and spaces that will be used. You can space out the letters somewhat to fill a line, or you can position them closely to fit a tight spot.

3. Use the tweezers to remove the letters, one at a time, from the backing. Position each letter, but do *not* press it down yet. Follow the ruled guideline (or set each letter against the bottom of your straight edge as a guide).

4. When you have the letters in exactly the correct position, then you can press them down, one at a time. Once these letters are pressed down, they are there for good. Carefully erase the guideline if it's showing anywhere.

Notepaper   23

How to make personal notepapers that people will remember

Just about every technique described in this book can be used to make notepaper. But, if you want to make your personal stationery in any quantity, use one of the methods that will allow you to produce a number of sheets easily. Silk screen printing is well suited to making notepaper as are the Styrofoam and linoleum block printing methods. Of course, you can use any of the techniques, and simply make the notepaper one at a time as the occasion arises. You might create a pattern for the needlepoint pen marking and just make your notepaper as it is needed. Such a sheet can be made in a few minutes if the pattern and color distribution are kept simple.

Although a greeting card frequently reflects the personality of the person who made or bought it, notepaper should be designed *specifically* to be *you*. You will want the notepaper to tell something about yourself. What are your hobbies? How about a favorite sport? You might consider using your astrological sign, your initials, or an ethnic motif if it has personal significance. A favorite flower or bird can be used as a design element, or a design can be created to illustrate a pet. You might even consider having a line drawing or a photograph of your home reproduced by a commercial printer.

Figure 23-1 illustrates several ways that notepaper can be folded to make it a little more interesting. These ideas are just starters. Think about a format yourself, but don't limit your ideas to the traditional rectangle. How about a sheet of notepaper whimsically cut in the shape of a foot, with the legend "footnote from   " printed on it (fig. 23-2)?

Think about using old-fashioned sealing wax to hold folds together. If you can carve a little, you might be able to make a seal from wood to use in the wax. Or, if there is a typesetter nearby, for very little money you should be able to have a line of display type set that you can press into the wax to leave the impression you want. The type is set in reverse so it will print correctly when pressed into the wax. And, believe it or not, you can still buy an initial letter seal. Check your local stationary store.

Plan your notepaper to fit standard envelopes, unless you want to make special size envelopes yourself (chapter 1 shows you how). You might consider buying plain notepaper and envelopes and decorating both the paper and envelopes with one of the methods we have described. Printing a design on the inside of the envelope, under the flap, is a nice touch. Consider repeating the pattern you have created for the sheet inside the envelope.

It's tempting to pick a colored sheet for notepaper, but if you do, keep the color light. The darker a sheet is, the more difficult

Fig. 23-1 Several ways to fold notepaper.

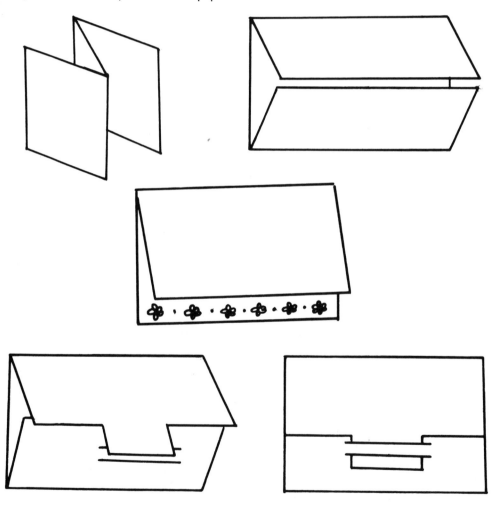

it will be for anyone to read the handwritten message. Pastel colors are the best bet for most notepapers.

Just about any paper can be used, but there are some sheets that will make better notepaper than others. If there is a commercial printer nearby, see if you can have some of his trim scraps when he is running an 80 lb English finish sheet. Trim scraps are often big enough so that you can cut your notepaper from them. If they were cut from a single job, these scraps will all be the same size, so the work of trimming them to size at home is simplified. A paper cutter is very useful for this.

Heavy bond typewriter paper can also be used for notepaper. It is produced in different colors, but you may have to order color sheets—they are seldom stocked by any but the largest stationery stores. Whatever you do, don't use any of the erasable papers. They are made with a waxy substance that makes them very difficult to use with any of the coloring and printing techniques we have described.

Figure 23-3 shows several ways to make notepaper, all based

Fig. 23-2 "Footnotes from . . . ."

Fig. 23-3 Several ideas for notepaper—and the possibilities are endless.

on techniques described in this book. Starting at the top and moving clockwise, the monogram is a cut-out made with three different colors of paper. The letters were interwoven and overlaid to enhance the design and to create a unified logo effect. The embossed gold initial was made from a conventional legal seal, which is available at most stationery stores. The marbled effect was created with oil and water. A separate sheet was printed with an oil and water pattern; then the sheet was trimmed and glued to the edge of the notepaper. The butterflies at the bottom were made with a Styrofoam block print. Ordinary shelf edge decals were positioned to make the note on the left.

As you can see, we have only scratched the surface. Making notepaper is truly a personal experience. Let your imagination go, and make a design that says *you*.

Printing Your Cards Commercially   24

How to work with a commercial printer

If you would like to produce a fair number of cards, but your time is limited, you might consider having your designs produced by a commercial printer. A common and relatively inexpensive short-run printing process (for a hundred to a thousand cards) is offset lithography. With offset printing, you can have simple line work reproduced as well as one-color drawings with variations in tone, and art with more than one color.

Offset plates are made photographically. The art to be printed is first reproduced as a film negative (shown on the right in fig. 24-1), and the negative is used to "burn" the plate. (An offset plate is shown on the left in the figure.)

Fig. 24-1 A film negative (right) is used to make an offset plate (left).

Offset is not the only printing process that can be used to print your cards. Many printers will have letterpress equipment which will give a comparable job, but the cost can be slightly higher because of the photoengraved plates that must be made. (The letterpress process is *not* limited to type.)

At one time, letterpress was the predominant method of printing, but the chances are that you will find more offset printers around and you will have greater flexibility with the offset process. For example, it is difficult and expensive to correct or replace a letterpress plate if an error has been made, but it is a simple and relatively inexpensive matter to burn a new offset plate if problems arise. For this reason, the process we discuss will be offset. But, before we get into the preparation of artwork for an offset printer, let's take a look at paper stock, envelopes, and ink.

Selecting Paper and Envelopes

Paper for offset printing is made so that the ink will soak in a bit as the impression is applied by the press. For this reason, it is best to avoid coated or glossy sheets—they just won't absorb the ink as well. Stick to a paper with an offset finish, or a dull coated sheet which has a slight sheen. Rely on the printer to help you make the best selection.

Paper comes in various weights, and you'll want to select the appropriate weight paper, or "stock," for your card. A 50 lb. or 60 lb. offset sheet is best if you are planning a French fold. This means that the card will be folded in quarters down to $4^1/4'' \times 5^1/2''$ (using $8^1/2'' \times 11''$ paper) and will fit in a standard number $5^1/2$ envelope ($4^3/8'' \times 5^5/8''$). If you want an unfolded card of the same dimension, use a heavier stock. Heavy stock is referred to as cover paper. Have the printer show you some cover papers if that's what you think you'd like to use.

Unless you are planning a commercial venture, it is best to plan your work for a simple press that accommodates a standard $8^1/2'' \times 11''$ sheet. This is an economical way to handle a hundred or so, or even as many as a thousand cards. If you want to print more than a couple of thousand cards, it may be more economical to use larger size sheets of paper on which several cards can be "ganged" and printed at one time. The larger paper will require a larger press.

You don't have to plan your printing to use every inch of a sheet of paper. You can design the card to suit your needs, and the printer can trim away any waste after the press run. A printer can trim paper any way you want by having a special die made, but this is a rather expensive step. It is better to have the printed card cut to shape, if necessary, on a commercial paper cutter. Just about any straight line can be cut on a commercial paper cutter. The job doesn't necessarily have to be square; the card can be cut in the shape of a triangle or any other linear format.

If your idea calls for a bleed, that is, color that runs off the edge of the paper, you will have to plan your design and select a larger paper size so that there will be room for trimming after the press run. This is because the press cannot print right to the edge of the sheet. Your design must extend about ¼" beyond the "trim line," which represents the actual dimensions desired for the finished card (see fig. 24-2). After the print run is over,

Fig. 24-2 Color which goes off the edge of the finished card is called a bleed. The card must be printed on a larger sheet and is then trimmed to size.

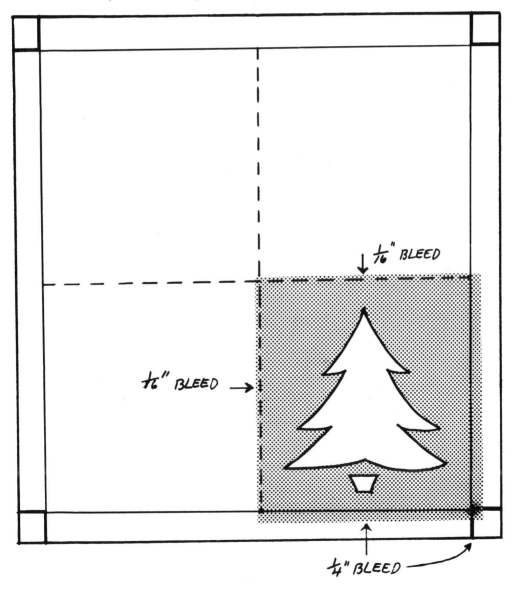

the sheets are cut to the trim line and the color runs off the edge of the paper.

You can add color to your card by printing on colored paper. But, remember that ink laid on a colored stock will not have the same hue as it does when it is printed on a white sheet. It's best to ask your printer for his advice—he may be able to provide you with a sample of the colored sheet with the ink on it before you commit yourself to the paper or the ink.

Although you can print any size and shape card you want, you should plan your card to fit in one of the standard envelopes (fig. 24-3). They are:

Commercial (No. 6¼)	3½″ × 6″
Official (No. 10)	4⅛″ × 9½″
Baronial (No. 5½)	4⅜″ × 5⅝″
Booklet (No. 7)	6¼″ × 9⅝″
Booklet (No. 063)	6½″ × 9½″
Booklet (No. 090)	9″ × 12″

A number of the paper mills make envelopes in some of the same colors used to make printing paper. If the idea of matching the paper and the envelope color appeals to you, ask your printer to show you some samples.

Fig. 24-3 Standard shapes of envelopes.

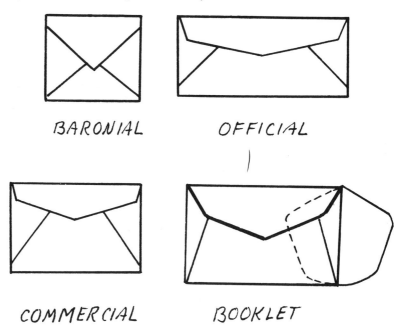

BARONIAL   OFFICIAL

COMMERCIAL   BOOKLET

Printing Inks

Printers describe jobs in terms of the number of colors used. A one-color job simply means that only one ink is used in a single press run. The ink may be black, or any color you want. Even if you print with one color and use a colored paper, it is still a one-color job. A two-color job is one on which two separate colors of ink are printed. For the small runs most cardmakers order, each color is printed separately on an individual press run. However, large runs of commercial quantity cards are printed on multi-color presses. One pass at the press is all that is required, but several colors are printed in a single operation.

Ask your printer to show you his ink sample book. Some of these sample books have many hundred different colors, but be careful to select a standard ink. Many of the colors must be mixed specially, and they are often sold in rather large minimum quantities that can be expensive. If you have a specific color in mind and have a sample, the printer can have his ink supplier match it—but, it, too, will be expensive.

Preparing Art for Offset Reproduction

Three kinds of art are readily produced on an offset press: line art, line art with gradations of tone in selected areas, and paintings reproduced in one color.

Line art. There are no gradations of tone in line art. A pen and ink drawing, or a drawing like that in fig. 24-4, is an excellent example, and such work can be reproduced easily on an offset press.

The early Currier and Ives prints were produced as line art, and color was added by hand after the press run. This is an easy way to produce a multi-colored card for very little money. The card we have chosen to illustrate this technique is one that we used as our Christmas card. Watercolor paint was added to the printed fireplace setting. See photo 18 in the color section.

Most of the techniques described in this book can be used to reproduce a limited number of cards. However, you can use some of them to produce prints that can be reproduced in larger numbers by offset lithography. For example, silhouettes, block prints, stencils, and monochrome pen marking can be used to produce single-color cards by offset. Two or more colors can be reproduced, too, but you must consider the cost of the additional plates and press runs.

Line art with tints. If you would like to add some areas of flat

Fig. 24-4 An example of line art.

tone (the same color as your ink) to your design, you can lay pre-printed screens on the artwork. These sheets, available in most art supply stores, are made up of patterns of dots (see fig. 24-5); the finer the dot, the less obvious it will be. The values of the tones are graded as percentages; the higher the percentage, the darker the tint. Thus, a 10% screen is very light and an 80% screen is close to being a solid. You can use screens of different values to create unusual effects in the tints.

The dotted screens have sticky backings, and they will hold in place when rubbed down. It's best to lay the sheet over the section to be toned and trim away the excess with an X-acto knife

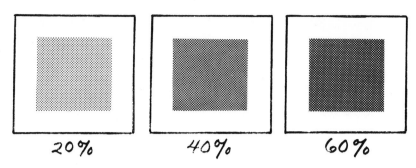

Fig. 24-5 Samples of screens.

(no. 11 blade) after you have rubbed the screen in place. These sheets are not inexpensive, so plan the placement and cuts carefully.

In fig. 24-6, a transparent overlay has been placed over the art and marked to indicate the placement for tints to enhance the appearance of the line card. Do not write on the art itself. Figure 24-7 illustrates the card with the tints rubbed down in place. This art can serve as "camera-ready" copy for the printer, and a negative and line plate can be made from it directly.

If you don't feel up to applying the screens yourself, you can have the printer do it. The printer will position the screen during the photographic process and will produce a negative with the appropriate tones in place. You will have to indicate on a tissue overlay just where the tint is to be positioned and what percentages you want (see fig. 24-6). The printer can help you select the percentages depending on how dark or light you want the tints to be.

When the screen is applied as we have described, the screen and the line work will print in the same color. But, if you would like to have the tint appear in a second color, the screen must be applied to an overlay on the art and the printer will make a separate plate for the color. This, of course, will cost more.

Wash drawings. When a painting is to be reproduced, the printer will make the plate as a halftone. That is, a special screen will be placed between the artwork and the film during the photographic process, and all of the tones will appear as tiny dots. To get an idea of how this works, use a magnifying glass to look at a photograph reproduced in a magazine. See how the dot intensity varies as the areas of the picture go from dark to light. Such a single shot, whether it is made of a monochrome wash drawing or a multi-color oil painting will print in one color only. In order to make a faithful reproduction of a many-colored painting, the four-color process must be used, but this is beyond the scope of this book and the pocketbooks of most amateur cardmakers.

Whatever kind of artwork you want to be reproduced on your card, it must be clear, clean, and distinct when you give it to the printer. Any fuzzy lines, smudges, and blemishes that are on the original are likely to show up on the printed card. You can clean up a line drawing with opaque white paint, or by using a razor blade to scrape away any material that is not to be reproduced.

Always ask your printer for a "proof" of the card. The proof is made before the card is printed, and you can check it for unwanted spots or other blemishes that you don't want to show on the finished card. And be sure to check to see that everything

Fig. 24-6 Line art with overlay indicating placement for tints.

you *do* want is there (it is possible for bits of printer's stripping tape to obscure part of the design). Clearly indicate on the proof what you want to be cleaned up. The printer is usually able to remove spots and smudges, but don't expect him to repair your fuzzy lines or fix anything that was faulty on the original art.

Printing a Lot of Cards

Short-run printing is expensive, from a cost-per-card point of view. For example, the offset-printed, hand-colored card of the fireplace shown in the color section cost $18 to print 100. That's 18¢ a card, admittedly less than you'd pay for even the simplest

Fig. 24-7 Line art with screens in place.

of commercial cards. But at a cost of 18¢ it would be difficult to make any money if the card were being made for sale.

However, as the quantity of the print run goes up, your total cost increases, but the cost per card goes down. This same card in a quantity of 10,000 copies might have cost less than a penny a piece. There are also savings to be made when buying larger quantities of paper. So, if you're making your card for sale, printing a large quantity can increase your profits, because your cost per card is low.

When planning large runs, it is important to size the job to the right press. Running 10,000 copies of this card on the press that was used for the short run would have been expensive and time-consuming. Such a large run is most economically printed as multiple impressions on a big press.

Reprinting Your Card

Offset plates usually oxidize and become unuseable after being stored for a while. However, the negatives can be kept for a number of years, and new plates can be made from them at any time. If you plan to re-run the card at a later date, ask for the negative and put it aside. (Be sure to tell the printer at the very beginning that you would like to keep the negative.) Keep it flat and in an envelope to protect it from being scratched. If you want to make minor changes to update your card, it is usually best to revise your original art and have a new negative shot.

Selecting a Printer

Unless you know a printer who does cards, either from your own experience or that of friends, look in the yellow pages. If the ad says the company prints offset, is a commercial printer, or prints brochures and the like, that printer is at least a candidate. Call him and ask if he can print cards. If not, ask him for recommendations of other printers who might be able to handle the project.

Be sure to get estimates of the cost so you can compare and select the best printer to fulfill your needs at the best price. When getting estimates, be sure to give each printer exactly the same information so that you will be able to evaluate their prices properly.

When you discuss the job with a printer and are asking for estimates, here are some points to keep in mind:

1. How many cards will be printed?
2. What is the finished (trim) size of the card?

3. What type of paper will be used? Ask the printer to show you various finishes in different weights and different colors. Remember that heavy paper is difficult to fold.

4. How many folds, if any, will there be? In what direction will the folds be made? Some heavy papers have a decided grain, and when folded against the grain, they will have an uneven edge. Ask the printer to run such paper with the grain to be sure that the cards can be folded properly.

5. What type of artwork will be used (line drawing, wash, photograph, painting, etc.)?

6. What color or colors will be used?

7. Will the ink coverage be heavy? A very strong background color may require two runs, although this is seldom a problem with amateur cards.

8. Will there be any tinted areas? Will you or the printer position them?

9. How about bleeds? Where will they be and on how many sides?

10. Will the card be printed on one or two sides? Remember that a French fold will give you printing inside and out on a *folded* card, but only one side of the paper is printed.

11. What's your schedule? How about the printer's schedule? If you have a tight timetable, be sure to let the printer know, and get a delivery date commitment.

12. What kind of proof will you want? A blueprint is fine for a card to be printed in one or two colors, but if you are using more color and registration is important, a color key might be requested.

13. Will the printer be able to supply the envelopes? If they are to match a colored paper, they will have to be ordered specially. Be sure to leave enough time in your schedule for such a special order.

14. What about foldouts, cutouts, and odd shapes?

Remember, when planning to print your cards by offset, the printer is your best adviser.

25   Patterns and Designs

A collection of motifs for most occasions

In making your own cards, you can use the designs that illustrate the various techniques described in previous chapters, or you can strike out on your own. To help you create your own greeting card designs, we have included here a number of adaptable patterns. The patterns represent a variety of motifs that can be the basic design elements of greeting cards for most occasions. You can trace these patterns directly and use them with whatever cardmaking technique you choose, or you can modify them to suit your own feelings.

Think about design. For example, use one pattern several times in a single design. The rhythm of repetition is an important design concept. Often, a more interesting design results when an illustration is placed off center on the card, not right in the middle. A very small pattern on a large field can attract considerable attention. Look at commercial greeting cards and you will recognize these and other techniques. See what approaches you like, and use them in your own work.

Think about the occasion. A softly curved pattern creates a gentle, restful mood. Designs with this feeling are ideal for such cards as baby announcements, religious holidays, and anniversaries. But patterns with straight lines and sharp angles have the opposite effect.

Think about color. Soft pastels go well with cards such as those created with flowers and those made with tissue paper. The quilled cards benefit from the use of pastels, too. Bright, vivid hues work well with block, Styrofoam, linoleum and silk screen printed cards. There are many rules for the use of color, but when making a greeting card, you can usually trust your own feelings. After all, you are trying to convey your own emotions to another person, and the chances are that the colors you select will complement the thought you have in mind.

The design you want just might not be in the following pages.

But if you thumb some magazines or newspapers, or look at the designs on some commercial greeting cards and gift wrapping, an idea just might suggest itself. If you like the idea, use it. But, if you would like to add something more, something that can only be said if you put your own touch to the pattern, we urge you to do it.

Most people who have not had any art training hesitate to do something on their own, and this is a mistake. You will be surprised at what you can do if you plan the project carefully, and work slowly to produce just what you want. Even if it isn't what you would consider professional, it does say what you want to say, and you did it yourself. This is the real meaning of a greeting card.

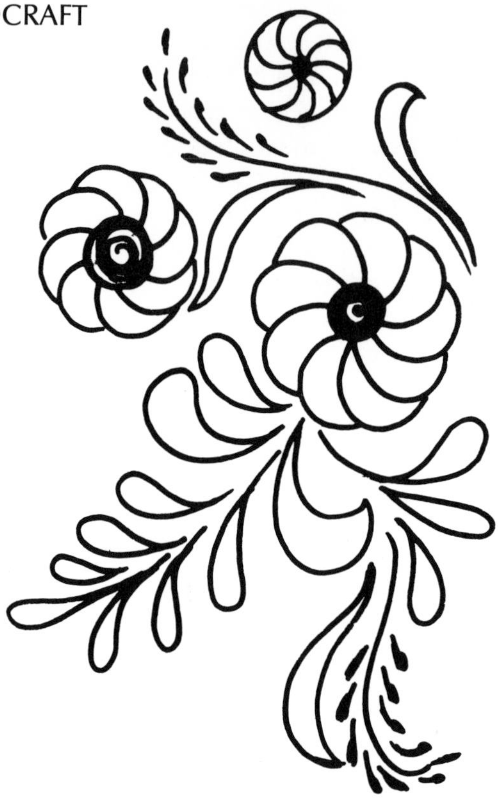

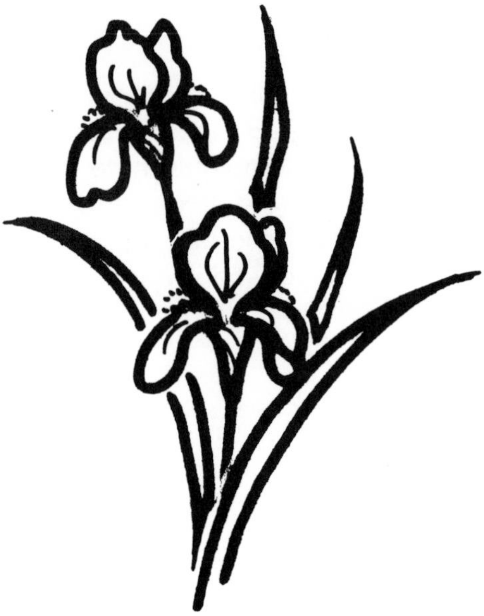

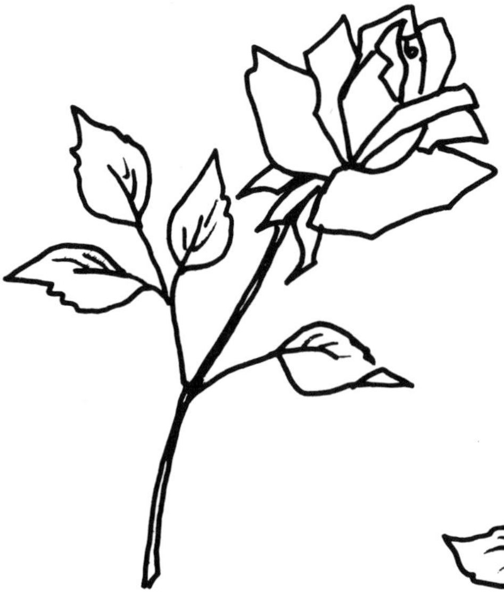

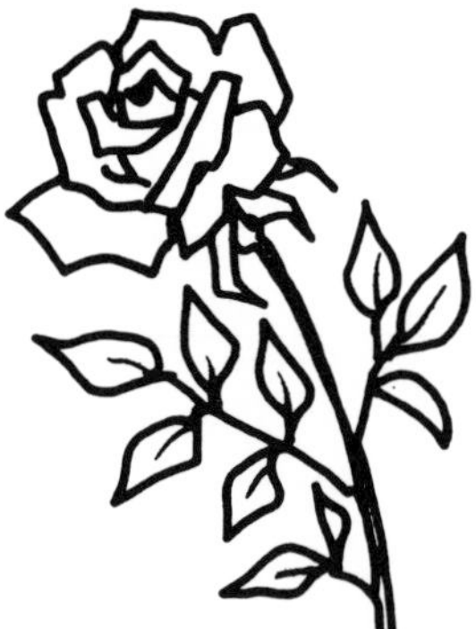

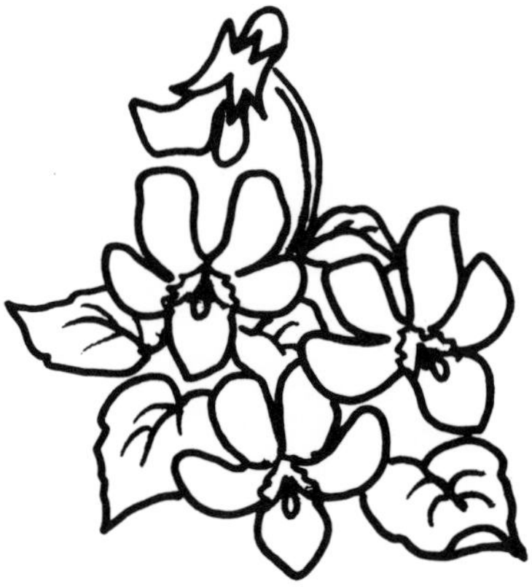

Sweet 16

BIRTHDAY